I'MPOSSIBLE

DESIRE. DREAM. DO.

Dianna,

It really is possible ☺

2024

JEFF GRIFFIN

i

I'Mpossible books may be ordered through booksellers or by contacting:
Griffin Motivation LLC
www.griffinmotivation.com
1 (801) 842-1213

Because of the dynamic nature of the Internet, any web addresses or links contained in this book may have changed since publication and may no longer be valid. The views expressed in this work are solely those of the author and do not necessarily reflect the views of the publisher, and the publisher hereby disclaims any responsibility for them.

The author of this book does not dispense medical advice or prescribe the use of any technique as a form of treatment for physical, emotional, or medical problems without the advice of a physician, either directly or indirectly. The intent of the author is only to offer information of a general nature to help you in your quest for emotional and spiritual well-being. In the event you use any of the information in this book for yourself, which is your constitutional right, the author and the publisher assume no responsibility for your actions.

Cover image provided by Shutterstock. © Shutterstock.

ISBN: 978-1-5043-3538-6 (sc)
ISBN: 978-1-5043-3539-3 (hc)
ISBN: 978-1-5043-3540-9 (e)

Library of Congress Control Number: 2015910093

Printed in the United States of America

Dedication

For Emily, the Love of my Life! My best friend and biggest fan! Without you I never would have walked down this path. Thank you for our beautiful four kids. Thank you for all the laughs and giggles.

For Bradley, Savanna, Karlee, and Katelyn. Always know and understand that anything is Possible if you include the Great I AM! Live the Laws of Life with exactness and you will see prosperity and joy spring up and shower down upon you. Develop talents to serve your God, family, friends, and self. Seek Truth and Discover Wisdom. Forgive Freely and Love Deeply. Get down on your knees and give thanks. Get back up and Keep Going Forward with Faith. And always remember to Enjoy the Journey!

For Terry and Kaylene. Thank you both for ALL you have done for me and being the best parents ever.

For Robert and Elna. Thank you for allowing me to be a part of your family and saying yes to your daughter's hand in marriage.

For everyone else who helped with this story…
THANK YOU so very MUCH!

Contents

FOREWARD

I was delighted when I first met Jeff Griffin on stage in Calgary Canada. I was touched by his story and moved by his passion. When he invited me to write this foreword I was honored to share to the world what I witnessed that day on the stage in Canada and what you too can experience by reading this book at home.

I have admired his incredible work and achievements, but more importantly I'm impressed with his tenacity to help people KNOW what they want. This book is an excellent resource in chasing down your dreams and desires. With his award winning book I'MPOSSIBLE: Desire. Dream. Do. Jeff Griffin has given hope to thousands of people that they too can overcome their personal Mount Everest. By following his 12 Mile Markers of practical suggestions, the reader can reach their Summit of life's challenges and see the panorama and possibilities to also reach their dreams.

I highly recommend this book. The reader will be transported with good humor through one of life's greatest challenges-- paralysis, to wheeling with joy and eventually walking through a life well lived. Yes, you may shed a tear or two, but you will also laugh with him as you journey with him toward incredible achievements. It will help motivate you to completion. It will help you develop a stronger character. It will help you overcome your challenges with a simple but powerful process. You will be inspired and you will think, I too can live my dream!

What I like about Jeff and his book is the ability to reinvent himself and the passion he has for helping others start a new conversations for their lives with bolder, brighter, and more colorful dreams. Jeff chose his own path of success even after being given a life-sentence from a wheelchair. He is consistently consistent in looking for what he can do instead of looking at what he can't do! This book helps you accomplish the things you want!

This books unfolds an amazing path that leads you to finish what you start. You will discover a process that you, the reader will soon experience for yourself and find the success you have been looking for all along. This inspired book is for all ages.

It's very rare that a book will come along and capture your dreams. It's even more rare that a book is constructed so you can orchestrate and conduct the song that sings in your soul. It will captivate your imagination and cultivate a passion that matches the desires of your heart. More importantly it is a book that is especially written to see your power and potentials magnified in chasing down your dreams. If you meet him, he will tell you just as his nurse at St. Benedicts Hospital told him "I don't care what others have told you. You can overcome this."
Desire, Dream, Do. Yes, I'Mpossible.

Raymond Aaron
New York Times Bestselling Author

BASE CAMP

Mount Everest
in All Her Glory

Introduction—Mount Everest in All Her Glory

The sun's rays filtered in from the partially opened shades of the plane. They lit up the world in front of me and warmed my soul knowing I was almost to my destination. The beautiful golden light replaced the gray and hazy cobwebs from my eyes revealing the most spectacular scene I have ever seen. I looked out the small 7-inch window and witnessed something I'll never forget! I beheld something in this magnificent world that the majority of people never get to see. I was looking out at Mount Everest, the world's highest peak.

I was at the tail end of a three-flight journey with two layovers in between, logging nearly 24 hours of flight time. I hadn't gotten any real sleep in the last 36 hours. My bloodshot eyes were heavy, my mind was slow and sluggish, and my body was even slower in response. "How did I get here?" I thought to myself. "Am I d-r-e-a-m-i-n-g?"

My ultimate dream is to run again, let alone stand. I dream that someday I'll take my wife on a walk in the park, hand in hand, side by side, and stride for stride. I see myself boxing out my son for a rebound, with a great hip-check, on the basketball court. I also see the day when I will give my daughters a piggy-back ride, or stand by their side as I give them away on their wedding day. The experts have told me straight to my face that this can't be done. This motivates me even more. Others keep telling me it's impossible. I tell them I'm possible! I know that with the right desire, determination, and power from above, the impossible becomes possible. I'm always telling myself and others that "If you can see it, you can achieve it." This attitude is one of the reasons I was invited to come to Nepal.

Our plane was at cruising altitude of around 30,000 feet,

and Mount Everest was the main focal point of the portrait framed in my window pane. Normally when I'm flying around the country I'm looking down at the mountains. Even the massive mountain ranges of Utah and Colorado are small from the vantage point of a plane. Not Mount Everest! It was massive and impressive.

Mount Everest, or as the locals call her, Sagarmatha, was sitting above the clouds at just over 29,000 feet. "I need to take a picture of this!" I thought. The thought slurred from my mind as I continued to soak up the scene that was playing out in real High Definition. The vision before me needed to be photographed but the beauty of the sparkling mountain peaks was too much for my exhausted body to respond to such a thought. I left the camera in the overhead compartment and just stared at the scene floating before my eyes.

The peak of Sagarmatha, which means "Goddess of the Sky," was not completely shrouded in its wardrobe of ice and snow. I could see the massive rocks from underneath the white cloak of snow and ice that couldn't be covered or conquered. Mount Everest was floating in the sky like a castle inviting weary travelers to come and take refuge. But it wasn't the only giant fortress in the sky that morning. In both directions I could see four or five similar pillars standing like sentinels protecting this portion of the universe. They seemed like floating buttresses ready to defend and protect against any and all evil that tried to get by. Perhaps I was looking at the mountain peaks of Lhotse, Makalu, Cho Oyu, or even K2. I briefly thought to myself how spectacular it would be to be a part of something so enormous, undaunting, majestic, beautiful, and some might even say inviting.

To most, Mount Everest isn't that inviting. In fact, until the early 1900s the general opinion was that it was impossible to climb and it couldn't be done. Then, the thought of conquering Mount Everest started to gain traction and take shape. The impossible might just be possible. In 1921 and 1922 a British expedition team with high hopes made two attempts to scale the 29,000-foot peak. They embarked on the climbs from the north side in Tibet. The mountain and elements were too much for them. They were beaten and dejected after two consecutive failed attempts. Conquering Mount Everest was still impossible! However, the two expeditions were not a complete failure. The second attempt proved to the world and to the team that human beings could push themselves further than before and higher than expected. Their trip was deemed unsuccessful by the experts, but to others they did something that had never been done before. They made it past 26,247 feet (8,000 meters), the first time any human being had climbed that high. Still the impossible was not quite possible in the eyes of the experts.

On June 8, 1924, the two-man team of George Mallory and Andrew Irvine attempted the final ascent to Mount Everest's summit. Mallory and Irvine disappeared from the view of those who stayed back at camp. No one knew that day as they entered the impenetrable veil of clouds, which separates the masses below from the majestic few above, that these two men would never return nor be seen alive again. The news of their deaths reached the critics and galvanized their certainty that the impossible feat of standing on top of the world would never be done by a human being. The debate was solidified and their argument would continue to rage on for another 30 years. It really was impossible!

It wasn't until 1953 that the impossible became possible. Edmund Hillary and his Sherpa guide Tenzing Norgay made the first official summit of Sagarmatha. They took a different, less-traveled path through the southern route of Nepal. They reached the top of the world! They conquered the mountain, tackled their fears, and silenced the experts. The impossible was achieved and Sagarmatha was summited.

Why were Hillary and Norgay able to accomplish that which was impossible for hundreds of others who tried but failed? How did they get to the top when others perspired but perished too? How was it possible to reach the top when the same odds were stacked against them? Where did they find the strength to attempt such a task when experts and evidence were screaming it couldn't be done? How did they get past the darkened difficulties and reach the top of the world and see the light?

I don't know the answers or understand their reasons, but I do know how I made it to the top of my Mount Everest.

When it comes to reaching the top of the world, Mount Everest, the majority of us now know it's possible. Our confidence has increased because the gear has gotten better, the dangers have been discovered, and the guides are greater than ever. We have hope because others who have gone before us inspire us. In 1988, Stacey Allison became the first American woman to do it. A 16-year-old Sherpa named Temba Tsheri did it in 2001, making him the youngest to ever do it. A blind man named Erik Weihenmayer did it as well—talk about seeing the world with a different vision. Gary Guller did it and he only had one arm. On May 23, 2013, an 80-year-old Japanese man did it, making him the oldest man to summit the Goddess of the Sky. In fact, one of my USA teammates, Jeff Glasbrenner, was the first American amputee to do it. They're possible!

The ping of the seatbelt light and the preparation for our descent into Katmandu brought me back to reality. It started to get darker and Mount Everest disappeared from view as we entered into the rain clouds. The reason for going to Nepal had a lot more meaning after see the Goddess in the Sky and I found it a little ironic that I wasn't coming to Nepal to climb Mount Everest. Instead, I was going there because I had already climbed my own Mount Everest. I was going there in response to an invitation to help the local disabled community. I arrived in Nepal ready and willing to show them the light that exists above the cloudy haze and struggles of life.

These citizens have been sitting in the shadows of society for years, if not decades, patiently performing life's mundane and menial tasks, willing and waiting to receive additional assistance. I was asked to bring tools of hope to tackle and achieve the "possible" that had been taken away or withheld from them for most of their lives. I wanted them to feel the joy and happiness that comes from climbing and conquering their own Mount Everest. I came with a clear and concise plan to prepare them for their own personal struggles and setbacks. I brought the essential resources of information and knowledge to remind them where they needed to go, how they needed to get there, and why they needed to begin immediately. I came to Nepal as a Sherpa of sorts, someone who had learned for himself what it takes to change the impossible into the possible. *I'm possible!*

Some of you may be thinking right about now that my experiences and my life have nothing to do with your problem(s) or with your life, especially since you probably aren't even in a wheelchair. Perhaps your opinion will change after reading this book and you'll see we aren't much different after all. Others of you may be thinking I don't understand or have a clue about what you're going through. You're right. I don't fully understand nor will I ever understand, but I do know there is One who does. I know He has gone before. I know He understands you, your world, and what you are personally going through. I have been graced with the understanding and knowledge that He knows and understands all of us individually and personally. We must accept His invitation to "come unto Him" and personally invite Him to be our guide. *He's possible!*

I believe we all have a handicap or a Mount Everest to climb in some area of our lives. Nobody is perfect, no matter how much you want to believe you are. Your handicap could be a mental disability that pains you beyond comprehension. It could be something you have been suffering for days, months, or even years. It could be a social handicap that paralyzes you in public or inside your private parapet. It could be a physical handicap like my own where others can instantly see your problems. Your handicap could even be a spiritual handicap you refuse to acknowledge. Whatever your individual handicap is, it can be conquered! Disabilities can be either debilitating or liberating. They can hold us back or lift us up. They can remain our weakness or they can become our strength.

I hope sharing my story of big dreams, grave disappointments, and euphoric triumphs will help in some small way to lift you closer to the light that lifts. With each passing mile marker along the journey we can learn from our experiences or be lost because of them. I have found peace in the pain and joy in the journey. I hope you can find some too as you embark on your own journey within the pages of this book. Remember, there are no excuses when it comes to creating success. *You're possible!*

I know from personal experience that most of us, if not all of us, have been told at some time in our lives that we can't do this or we can't do that. We've been told the impossible is the only possibility in our lives. We've been told this enough times we start to believe the possible is truly impossible. Stop it! Take a breath and know you can achieve and overcome. I wholeheartedly believe we can. Eliminate the phrase "I can't" from your vocabulary unless you use it with "I can't right now, but I will." I would like to remind you of this "possibility principle" coined so well by the famous American author Ralph Waldo Emerson. He said:

> *"That which we persist in doing*
> *becomes easier for us to do;*
> *not that the nature of the thing itself is changed*
> *but that our power to do is increased."*

Possibility Principle
www.griffinmotivation.com/possibility

I invite you to write this quote down yourself, but do it with your nondominant hand. If you are right-handed do it with your left hand, and if you are left-handed do it with your right hand.

_____

_____

_____

_____

During our early childhood development days, we were formally taught how to copy the dotted lines from each letter of the alphabet. We were then taught how to put those letters together to form words. Once we learned the words we were encouraged to form sentences with those words. I'm sure if you are like me, it's been a long time since you've even thought about how you learned how to write. When we began learning how to write we probably didn't even think it was a daunting task. We didn't think it was impossible, we simply accepted the fact that we were going to learn how to do it. It wasn't easy at first, but we worked at it and it got easier. For most of us we became better at it, not because writing changed and became easier, but because we persisted in doing it. In the same way, we can do new things today. Not that it will be easy, but because we will persist in doing what needs to be done.

As Lao and Confucius once said, "A journey of a thousand miles begins with one step." This book is about taking that journey one step at a time. It's about dreaming and accomplishing the impossible. It's not only about aiming for the sky and reaching for the stars, but enjoying the journey along the way. Begin your personal journey, press forward to the top, and don't you ever stop. As you move toward your dreams, there will be obstacles and setbacks along the way, but don't be afraid. If you do get lost, do as the mariners of old did and look up to someone who knows and regain your bearings. If you follow the signs with exactness you will discover that there really is a certain way to gain success and progress. You will find success in things like promotions, raises, million-dollar ideas, solving past problems, finding simple solutions, discovering new relationships, rekindling old ones, mending marriages, losing weight, opening the door to new opportunities, and finding fresh and exciting possibilities!

I truly believe in order to progress to success in life we must first find out who we really are. If we know who we really are we can do what we really need to do and then we can become what we are really supposed to be: Great! If you're still not sure you can make the impossible possible and truly become great, I am here to tell you that you can. Right now, if you don't believe in you, I believe in you! You can get your dream job. You can build your life on a solid foundation. You can set goals and work smart. You can forgive. You can achieve your dreams. You can lose pesky pounds. You can give back and serve. You can be kind all the time. You can give credit where credit is due. You can get to the top of your world if you sincerely do it with the right desire and take the proper steps. You can do it with me. You can do it with others. We can do it together, one step at a time. *We're possible!*

To make the "possible" happen, I invite you to commit to three simple steps:
1) Pay attention to the quiet impressions that will come to your mind.
2) Follow the small "signs" of instruction from this book; they will help you in the biggest ways.
3) Promise yourself you will follow through and do the things you feel, see, and learn.

Signature_____

Date_____

MILE MARKER 1

Day of Shattered Dreams

Mile Marker 1–Day of Shattered Dreams

It was a bright beautiful summer morning back in 1995. We had work to do and it was a perfect day to do it. Gazing up toward the top of the barn and looking into an expanse of light blue sky, I noticed the few wispy clouds that accented the wonderful possibilities that dotted my own future.

"I will be successful," I thought as I laboriously climbed up the ladder to do the job some doubted I could do. I had been painting all summer and business was booming. I had just contracted to paint an enormous old barn and with this one and others it was more than a 22-year-old, one-man owner could handle. I desperately needed some help, so I hired my good friend Doug. For the next three days, we would be painting a barn in Preston, Idaho, which would put us directly in *Napoleon Dynamite* country. Preston was a 45-minute drive from my hometown of North Logan, Utah. I was excited to get this job started.

This particular job brought me hope and excitement because when I finished painting the barn, I would have enough money to purchase the motorcycle I had always wanted: a 1995 Honda CBR 600 F3 red, white, and blue four-stroke "ladies machine." With a 100 horsepower 12,000 revolutions per minute (rpm) engine, it could get from 0 to 60 miles per hour in about 4 seconds, topping out at over 140 mph. That was enough power and speed for any junky. It was a dream come true and a mom's worst nightmare. There would also be enough money left over for my upcoming year of college without having to work. This would allow me to be totally focused on football, girls, and school…in that order.

That morning I had loaded up the truck with my painting equipment and picked up my new employee. Doug and I headed off to Preston. The journey was going great until we crossed the Utah/Idaho border and ran into road construction. The next 12 miles was bumper-to-bumper traffic.

"Who would have thought there could be this much traffic in farm country?" I asked, trying to break the silence.

"I didn't know there were this many people who wanted to get into Idaho," Doug rhetorically responded.

We really didn't mind the traffic. And we weren't going to let it get us down nor get us in a bad mood. In fact, it gave us a chance to talk about the important things of life: football and girls! We reminisced about last year's undefeated 11-0 football season at Ricks College, and our years playing football for Sky View High School and the girls who came to the games. We talked about the possibilities for the Ricks football team and all the pretty girls who would be there. We talked about the fact that I would be leaving home soon and heading up to Rexburg, Idaho, where I would find the beautiful young ladies, in just a few weeks. Once we finished with the topics of football and girls we got to the most exciting topic at hand: bungee jumping. Yes, bungee jumping. I had never been and I was going to go that night for a young adult activity. I was ecstatic. And of course, there were going to be ladies there.

Doug and I finally arrived at the job site. Unfortunately, we had lost a couple of hours of good light and cool weather because of the road construction. I had no worries though, we would make up for it. I was sure of that. I pulled the old but reliable 30-foot ladder out of the back of the truck while Doug started unloading the scaffolding. The back of the truck was quickly stripped of its contents. With the 5-gallon paint cans to the side and the paint sprayer out of the way, the task of putting the scaffolding together began. Millions of construction workers, painters, and building maintenance crews work on scaffolding every day, and due to the nature of its use, scaffolding must be properly constructed and used to ensure the safety of those who use it. Many large commercial and government construction projects require all workers to have scaffold training and be OSHA certified. I apparently didn't get the memo on that requirement. Our job was going to be a simple one-day use of the scaffolding. It was not like other complex construction jobs you see in big cities. Our setup was both simple and rudimentary.

One level of scaffolding was finally complete. We connected the crossbars and fastened them together to the corners of the poles with cotter pins. We inserted the perimeter poles of the scaffolding into the four foundational plates. Each 1-foot-square plate provided the safety and support needed as we tipped the scaffolding to its vertical position. Once positioned next to the barn, we laid a couple of 2x8 wooden planks across the top of it so the 30-foot ladder could be placed on top of that. I scampered up the 8-10-foot climb to the top of the scaffolding in no time. Doug hoisted the ladder up to me and I solidly placed the ladder on the wooden planks. The legs of the ladder felt solid and secure against the wooden planks as I gently leaned the ladder against the big white barn.

"It's not even close to reaching the top," shouted Doug, trying to be helpful.

The ladder only reached two-thirds of the way up. We still lacked another 10 to 15 feet to reach the top.

"Thanks, Doug," I sarcastically replied. "I can see that."

I pulled the ladder back from the barn and quickly lowered it down to Doug. I hurried down from the scaffolding to retrieve the second level of scaffolding. We immediately went to work putting the second level of scaffolding together. After we completed our handy workmanship, we lifted the second level of scaffolding above the first and gently lowered it on top of the original. The second level of scaffolding connected perfectly with the first. This additional level added another 8 to 10 feet to our criss-crossed metal foundation. We put some more 2 x 8 wooden planks on top of that and copied the earlier process of placing the ladder against the barn. It still didn't quite reach the top. It didn't concern me too much though because the pressure from the paint sprayer would probably reach the top without having to raise the ladder any higher.

With the construction of the scaffolding and placement of the ladder complete, the real work was ready to begin. I asked Doug if he would hold the ladder for me at the top of the scaffolding. Doug hated heights, but he hesitantly complied. I grabbed my sprayer and Doug and I started up the scaffolding. Once on top, Doug stayed behind and held the ladder while I continued up it. As I began the climb I noticed Doug was shaking nearly uncontrollably. It caused the ladder to rattle with noise as the cold metal vibrated against itself.

"Are you sure you can handle this, Doug?" I asked nervously. "Because if not, I can give you a second to settle down and collect your emotions, you pansy!"

"I'm okay," came the quick reply. "And by the way, who's calling who a pansy?"

I slowly started to climb up the ladder, step-by-step-by-step-by-step…. Midway to the top I half-jokingly shouted down to Doug, but mostly with the intent to calm him down, "You know Doug, we could relate this to life: step-by-step; precept upon precept; here a little there a little…"

Before I could finish my sentence, Doug shot back jokingly but a little more serious: "Shut up Griff. Stop preaching to me!"

This seemed to loosen Doug up a bit and we both laughed about the exchange as I continued to the top.

I got as high as I could "safely" go on the ladder (once you are up 40 feet in the air without any rope, "safely" really is a relative phrase) and I could see that painting the top of the barn was going to be a challenge. I was hoping the pressure from the paint compressor would shoot the paint high and far enough to compensate for the lack of not being close enough to the top.

I lifted my arm above my head with the intent to spray the highest point of the barn first. With the sprayer in hand I squeezed the lever.... Just then, the unexpected happened. The paint dribbled out the nozzle and dropped down to the ground. I definitely knew I wouldn't be painting the top of the barn with this setup. Before descending, I looked up, breathed in, and became aware of the dazzling blue sky and the beauty all around us. Life was good and the remaining few months of 1995 were going to be the best.

I quickly and carefully descended the ladder and scaffolding and hurried over to the paint sprayer. Doug came down as well. He inhaled deeply and breathed normally for the first time since we started. I adjusted the sprayer and tested it out to make sure it would work this time. Sure enough, it was working like a charm. I motioned to Doug with my head, and said, "Let's do this!"

We both climbed back up the scaffolding to the base of the ladder. Instead of instantly going up the ladder, I decided to raise it one more notch. I wasn't going to leave it to chance or to the paint sprayer to paint the top of the barn. I didn't want to come back down from those heights again without having it painted and completed. To avoid a long and awkward wrestling match with the ladder, Doug and I pulled it back from the barn together. We struggled to keep our own balance while standing on the wooden planks, but we finally raised it and gently put it back in place against the side of the barn. This time I was positive I would reach the top and finish the job. I started up the ladder, and Doug resumed his position holding it. Fortunately for both of us, this time he wasn't shaking. Carefully putting one foot in front of the other, I slowly climbed. With every rung of the ladder behind me it brought me one step closer to finishing what I started. The excitement of getting the high parts over with started to percolate from within. I didn't enjoy being up there any more than Doug did.

The sun was heating things up fast and the ladder was warm to the touch. "We need to get things going," I impatiently thought to myself as I put one hand in front of the other and started my climb.

As I reached the halfway mark of the ladder Doug decided to get back at me for our earlier exchange.

"Hey Griff, I know you're excited to go bungee jumping tonight but I want to remind you that you don't have a cord," he said teasingly.

Jabbing back in return I said, "Shut up Doug! Stop preaching to me!"

We both laughed. We were a couple of comedians thinking how funny we weren't. I continued up the ladder. This time I was nearly 40 feet in the air and a foot closer to the top, my paint sprayer was working, and there wasn't anything that was going to keep me from doing this job.

"I'm here," I thought. "Let's get this over with and get back down to a safer position."

Again, I lifted my arm above my head and was about to squeeze the paint lever. Just then, what I didn't expect to happen, did! The genesis of total chaos. It was that infamous feeling every school kid has experienced at one time or another when you're leaning back on your chair after your teacher has repeatedly told you to sit down on all four legs. That feeling you get when gravity takes over and you slip. That feeling you get when your stomach lurches up to your throat, falls down to your feet, and then settles back again in its original place. That was it.

"Ahh shhhooot," I calmly thought as I let go of the sprayer. "I've got to do something quick or else!" I was having this conversation in my head. Everything was happening so fast that I didn't have time to speak outloud. The ladder swayed back and away from the barn. It slipped away from my feet, leaving me vulnerable from the metal perch I was previously standing on. "I so don't want to think about the 'or else'!" were my last thoughts.

Some loft doors were at the top of the barn where the ladder once rested. Earlier that day they had been closed for my painting project, but there remained a 1-inch gap between the doors. As I began to fall, I instinctively jammed my thumb into the gap and tried to hold on to the door as the ladder and scaffolding tumbled to the ground. For the split second I was dangling in the air I could hear metal crashing against metal as the ladder and scaffolding collapsed and crumbled on top of each other. As the dust began to settle around the pile of scrap metal, the muscles in my hand weakened from exhaustion and my grip slipped from the loft door. My thumb was yanked out of the gap, filleting the top part of it off. There was nothing I could do and my descent toward the heap of twisted metal and hard ground continued once again.

After letting go, while still falling, I noticed a 1-inch wooden ledge sticking out from the bottom of the loft doors. "Grab that ledge," I commanded myself. I reached out to grab it and I got lucky! My fingers came into perfect contact with the ledge. I gripped onto that ledge with all my might. I wasn't going to let go. No way! No how! Not now! But God had a different plan. The weight of my body and the pull of gravity were just too much for my fingers to bear. It caused my fingers to pop off the ledge. I was on my way down again and picking up momentum. I needed to think of something fast but what could I do? Just then a solution came to my mind I learned as a little boy watching Saturday morning cartoons. It was the Wile E. Coyote trick. I began clawing at the barn frantically with both hands, trying to make it back up to safety.[1] Wile E. Coyote's creators, Hanna Barbara failed me and I knew my fall was coming to an end, and fast.

My only and last option was to break my fall by absorbing the impact. This was going to be done by timing the speed of the fall with the oncoming ground. At the perfect time, I would have to bend my knees, collapse my body, and roll. I was planning on executing my plan the best I could and hoping for as little physical damage as possible. After all, many past experiences prepared me for this moment. There were the times my older brother sent me flying through the air as he sent me sailing from the trampoline to the ground. Somehow, I always managed to break my fall without getting hurt. I knew this was going to hurt but I was quite confident I would walk away from this one too.

"This is it," I said to myself as I prepared to look down at the fast-approaching ground.

What happened next took place in slow motion. I cocked my head to the side and bent my neck forward toward the ground to gauge the landing. Then it happened! As soon as I looked down, I was there. Unable to react at all, I hit the

---

[1] At the time I didn't remember doing that, but when I got to the hospital and things started to settle down I had a chance to examine my wounds. I noticed there were paint chips and wood splinters jammed underneath my fingernails where I had clawed the front of the barn.

ground straight-legged. I stuck the landing perfectly! If I were a gymnast I would have given myself a perfect 10. Unfortunately, I wasn't a gymnast. In fact, there was no spotter, no soft mat, nothing; just the solid ground and me. The force of the fall jarred my legs up toward my head, while the upper part of my body was still coming down. They both met at the L1 (First Lumbar) vertebrae of my spine, causing it to explode into what I thought was a million pieces, like a china dish hitting the floor.

The explosion ran down my legs, up my arms, and out my body like an underground mine explosion. The pain was excruciating. I have nothing to compare it with and to this day, I've never felt it since. As I collapsed to the side and crumpled to the ground I reached down and grabbed my legs. The pain in my legs hurt so bad that I instinctively grabbed one leg to eliminate or at least reduce the pain. As I clutched my leg in agony, my hand could feel my leg, but my leg could not feel my hand. The barn began to spin and the clouds in the sky began to tumble down and around. The enormity of the situation began to sink in. Right then and there I knew something bad had happened.

By this time, Doug had recovered from his own fall. Fortunately for both of us there was no damage done to him. He rushed over to me and while shaking me back and forth by the shoulders he cried out, "Jeff are you okay? Are you okay Jeff?"

Rocking back and forth I looked up at Doug and calmly said, "I don't think you should be doing that."

He stopped shaking me and gathered his senses. He stared down at me in shock and disbelief. I looked up into his panic-stricken eyes and with tears streaking down my cheeks I told him the bad news. "Doug, I think I'm paralyzed."

"You can't be," he replied with numbness.

"No, Doug, I really think I'm paralyzed. Call 911!"

Without hesitation Doug jumped up, ran to our client's house, and dialed 911.

Doug was gone and I was alone. I was hurt. I was a little frightened. I had just fallen 40 feet and had done something bad to my body. I didn't know what exactly, but I knew it was serious. I had just fallen 40 feet and my dreams had fallen with me. I knew my dream of riding my brand-new motorcycle was dashed to pieces. I also knew my dream of playing college football was over as well. My body was broken. My spirit was crushed. My dreams were shattered in an instant. I was heartbroken. I wasn't quite sure what to think at that moment. That dreaded question we all have asked before entered my mind, "What now?"

Have your dreams been shattered in the past? Have you stopped dreaming of the future? Have you been burned and made a fool of before? Have you suppressed your dreams because of fear or doubt? Is your heart tired of trying? If so, I invite you to dream again, to dream anew today! Get back up and move forward. Fill your heart and mind full of new dreams. Make a list of all the things you truly want to do and call it your Dream Bucket List!

Dream Bucket List

1._____

2._____

3._____

4._____

5._____

www.griffinmotivation.com/bucketlist

Early years dreaming about football.

MILE MARKER 2

True Desires

Mile Marker 2–True Desires

The sun pounded down on me as I lay on the ground in a blanket of weeds and grain. Beads of sweat started to percolate and roll down my forehead. Each new drop found the perfect path the previous one had left to follow. One by one the beads of sweat dripped off my forehead, rolling past my ear, and falling softly onto the dusty ground below. I had received a one-two punch from Mother Nature. The fall had shattered my dreams and now I too lay broken and left alone not knowing what would come next in the near or distant future. Lying on the ground in an empty field on the outskirts of town with nobody else around for miles, I waited for Doug to return. This moment by myself gave me the opportunity to reflect and ponder the time when my dream first germinated.

Ever since I can remember I dreamt about playing football for the Brigham Young University (BYU) Cougars in Provo, Utah. They were known for their incredible quarterbacks: Gifford Nielsen, Marc Wilson, Jim McMahon, Steve Young, Robbie Bosco, and Ty Detmer to name a few. They were a passing school and I was a receiver. We were made for each other.

Like most little boys, I had a dream of becoming somebody great and special. A lot of my friends dreamt about being a firefighter, a police officer, and even a soldier. Some wanted to become a doctor, a teacher, and others a lawyer. I on the other hand wanted to be an athlete. To help accomplish this dream, I thought I needed a poster on my wall. The only problem was I couldn't afford one when I was that young. In fact, my room at home was dreadfully bare and undecorated but at least the walls were white and clean. I shared my room with my little brother. We both were poor as church mice. We had nothing to put in our pockets, let alone on the walls. I was the fifth of eight children. I had an older brother and three older sisters who tortured me and kept me on my toes. I in turn tortured my younger brother and two younger sisters and kept them on their toes. It was the process of the pecking order being lived to its fullest.

My dad worked three jobs to keep the family fed and sheltered. His main source of income was made as a high school math teacher. Mom stayed home as a homemaker. She raised us to respect each other, to be patient with those less fortunate, and to honor our freedoms and our country. She strongly encouraged us to receive a higher education. We didn't have the material riches others around us had, but we grew up with a plethora of enduring treasures such as love, kindness, work, play, laughter, and plenty of good-natured teasing. The money thing didn't bother me until later in life when I went through that selfish stage known as the teenage years.

I never had too many toys, clothes, or other material items growing up because of the sheer number of siblings I had and the amount of money we didn't have. Nothing ever lasted, either. Whenever I received a gift or toy from somebody on Christmas or on my birthday, it would be ruined or taken away before it could be fully appreciated. When the day came that I received a poster from one of my friends, I ran downstairs and immediately put it on the back side of our bedroom door before it could get into the hands of my brothers or sisters.

It instantly brought life to our room and I loved it. It was a poster of Jerry Rice jumping over the San Francisco 49ers Candlestick Park stadium. It was a poster for my dream and the desire of my heart. I wanted to play football when I grew up. Before falling asleep at night, I would look at the poster and envision myself in Jerry's shoes running routes, catching passes, and making big plays. I wanted to be like him in every way as a receiver.

Up, down…up, down…up, down…went the tattered football as I threw it up in the air. When my friends couldn't play catch with me I would repeatedly play catch with myself in the quiet reaches of my basement. I would toss the football in the air and imagine the day when I too would be in a magazine or on a poster of my own. I would play games and begin challenging myself to see how close I could get the ball to the ceiling without hitting it. My mother never complained about all the marks on the ceiling. I don't think she ever saw them, but I do know she heard them.

"Stop hitting the ceiling with that ball," her voice would trail off as it found its way down to where I was lying on the floor.

Like most of Mom's requests it was ignored. The next toss of the ball barely missed the ceiling, defying gravity for that split second, and then returning softly to my hands. If the ball was near my hands, I would catch it. I learned that focusing on the cross-hairs and watching the ball all the way into my hands increased the percentages of catching the ball no matter the distractions around me. I learned this trick by doing it but heard about it from Hall of Fame receiver Steve Largent of the Seattle Seahawks. I studied every great receiver of my time to find out what their trick was and what they did to make them a great football player. My desire was to be great too.

Other times I would play catch while lying under the canvas of a clouded sky. Wherever it was, I would dream of the day when I would play for my favorite college team, the BYU Cougars. I imagined myself standing on the field in front of all the wild and crazy blue-painted fans. I could hear the deafening and exhilarating noise from the 67,000 fans simultaneously erupting with excitement and screaming their approval as I caught pass after pass from the next All-American quarterback. This type of daydreaming went on for years until one day my boyhood dream came one step closer to reality.

It was a sunny afternoon during the fall semester of my senior year in high school. I came home from a typical day of school when I saw it! My heart skipped a beat. There it was, sitting on the table waiting for me. My heart began to beat a little faster and a little harder. It was a letter from the legendary Hall of Fame coach, Lavell Edwards. Hoping I wasn't seeing things, I slowly inched my way toward the table, never taking my eyes off the envelope. Realizing it wasn't a dream, I dropped my backpack on the floor, bolted toward the table, and within five giant steps I was directly over the letter.

This is what I'd been dreaming about my whole life: an invitation and an opportunity to play football for the Cougars as a receiver! I reached down and picked up the letter, tore open the envelope, and looked inside. I couldn't believe this was happening. I was in disbelief because I'd been told my whole life that I couldn't do *it*. I wasn't fast enough, I wasn't strong enough, I wasn't tall enough, I wasn't good enough, I wasn't smart enough, I wasn't "enough" of this and I wasn't "enough" of that. Enough was enough. I was tired of the criticisms and excuses and this was my opportunity.

I remember telling someone my junior year in high school that I wanted to play football for BYU. I remember it like it was yesterday. I had just finished third period English and my classmate and I were walking out of the classroom discussing the topic of the day and he asked, "What do you want to do when you graduate?" I mentioned that I wanted to play football in college. Instead of getting some support like "that's cool," all I received was an incredulous look, a scoffing laugh, and a discouraging comment. "You'll never make it Griff, you're not good enough."

Negative and discouraging remarks happened back then, they still happen today, and they will continue to happen in the future. Fight the urge to listen to these voices and learn how to ignore them. We were not created to have others decide for us and determine what we should or should not do. All of us have been given the ability to choose for ourselves. What we do with our opportunities will eventually determine who we become. Every individual has the power and ability to choose what to do with that moment. There's a saying I learned as a boy that gave me strength to choose the right choice and listen to the right voice. "What matters most to you, you choose. What matters least to you, others choose for you."

This adage was important to me. I knew others would have their opinions and more times than not they would try to persuade me to believe it couldn't be done. They would try to get me to adopt their own limitations and doubts. They would try to persuade me to think like they did. They would try to convince me that good was bad and bad was good. I learned that comments about limitations and negative persuasions that came from my peers were powerful and persuasive. But I also learned I was in control of my own destiny, not my classmates, colleagues, friends, or family. It was my desire, my dream, my choice, and I had the power to do something about it.

"Open it!" My little brother poked my leg and prodded me back to reality.

I opened the envelope, took out the letter, and started reading. I couldn't contain myself any longer.

"I get to go to Provo and visit the campus!" I shouted. "I get to meet LaVell Edwards!" My voice was getting louder and the excitement in the air was contagious. My little brother was right there with me, jumping up and down and shrieking with joy and excitement. My celebration continued for a little while longer as I was wishing the whole world could hear me now. "I get to watch an in-state rivalry game," I continued to tell Chris. "We're going to kill them!"

I read it over and over, not really believing I actually received a letter from BYU. I devoured the words that appeared on the embossed letter. I even outlined the signature of Coach Edwards with my index finger. It felt good that someone had finally recognized I was a talented football player and I was good enough to play at the next level.

I put the letter back in the envelope and headed out the door. "My friends will be so jealous," I mumbled to myself. "I've got to go show them this letter."

Running up the street toward their houses and grinning from ear to ear, one last thought popped into mind as I approached the door. "They're never going to believe me."

I was both surprised and wrong about their reactions. My friends were supportive and excited about my news.

"When did you get the letter?" "What does it say?" "Do you get a scholarship?" Can we still be friends?" "Will you be sure to remember us little guys when you make it big?"

They put on their best smiles and enjoyed the short-lived moment of happiness with me but they also wanted to let me know I wasn't immune from practice.

"Griff you better watch your back at practice tomorrow—we're coming after you now!"

"Your mama can't save you tomorrow!"

"You'll need a lot more than a letter from LaVell to get respect from me!"

The good-natured razzing kept coming from each of my friends, and together we enjoyed the beginnings of my dream.

My family was just as excited for me as my friends were. talked about the possibilities around the dinner table. Dinner was a little less chaotic that night. Instead of fighting for the tator tots and fish sticks and grabbing whatever we could reach, I actually passed and asked for the food. Mom and Dad were really excited because they too would be meeting with the coaches and seeing the game.

The day finally came when my parents and I went to Provo and met with the coaches. Coach LaVell Edwards and Coach Chris Pella, the receivers coach, sat down with us and talked about the possibilities and their expectations.

Talking with LaVell Edwards and Coach Pella was a great honor and a wonderful experience. Seeing their facilities and getting a better picture of their program was a once-in-a-lifetime experience. However, I thought the best option and fastest way to get some playing time would be going to their junior college to play.

Ricks College was a much smaller school than BYU so I thought I would get plenty of playing time. I thought for sure my 46 catches, 9 touchdowns, and 839 yards in 10 games that year would merit the respect to propel me into a starting position or at least a chance to play.

It was August and time to report to football camp. I went a week early so I could run some routes with the veterans who were already there and prepare some more. I wanted to gain as many advantages as possible. Unfortunately for me, the other receivers who were reporting to camp had the same idea and the same resume. My plan of making a starting position wasn't as easy as I expected. In fact, it was worse than expected. Once I got there I realized I wasn't the proverbial big fish in the small pond anymore. In fact, I was just another fish in a bigger pond. I quickly realized I didn't come prepared as well as I thought I did.

In high school I was slow for a receiver but I made up for it by running perfect routes. I rarely focused on my speed because I had the best hands around. I would catch everything that was thrown to me. My hands didn't disappoint me. I could always rely on them. They were like Velcro to a felt ball. I figured my soft hands would carry me through the college season even if my heavy feet didn't carry me down the field as fast as the coaches and I would like. I wasn't ready for the negative comments that would come from my coaches, and I wasn't prepared for the criticism that came from my peers either.

"Griff, you're going too slow. Speed up!"

"Griff, you run like a white guy!" (How does a white guy run?)

"We only have four seconds to run this play, not all day."

Looking back, my teammates were just stating the facts but I took those comments personally and wouldn't let go of them. I continued to dwell on them play after play and series after series. I wasn't getting the touches I was used to in high school. Teammates weren't smacking my shoulder pads and giving me high-fives anymore. Guys were worried about themselves and if they could get rid of one more body, that would be one less person to compete against. This affected my focus and concentration. I repeatedly dropped balls that were thrown right to the numbers. I began thinking about dropping the pass instead of catching the pass. When I approached the line of scrimmage I would be thinking the negative half of the situation: "Don't drop the ball, please don't drop the ball." My focus had shifted. Since I was thinking of the negative aspect of not catching the ball, I received the negative outcome as a result. I was living proof that the law of attraction was real.

I thought I was stronger than that. I started to play with

doubt and fear. I allowed them to enter my mind without much resistance. Unfortunately, if you give doubt an inch, it will take a mile. Doubt is cancerous. Doubt is like that unwelcomed guest who will not leave your house once it enters. The only way to get rid of it is to be forceful and kick it out because it won't leave by itself.

I came to Ricks with high hopes of playing on the first team, but after the first day of practice I knew I was in for a long season from the bench–if I made it that far. I even began entertaining the possibility of quitting right from the start. I was physically strong, but mentally weak. I had failed before I even showed up. I was taught a valuable lesson at that moment: "If you fail to prepare, prepare to fail."

Because of my weak mental attitude and my poor thinking habits, the coaches would yell, teammates would sneer, and my confidence plummeted. I was no longer the stud receiver I thought I was and whom everybody loved in high school. I started listening to the voices of criticism. I began to be the "you're not good enough" person everybody said I was. I let other people's opinions matter more than my own. I allowed their comments to dictate my performance. I didn't understand yet that it's not a matter of opinion but *whose* opinion that matters.

It simply began by heeding the comments from teammates and coaches. The continued criticism captivated my focus and cultivated seeds of doubt on and off the field. The lack of focus had a major effect on my performance. This in return added more fuel for more comments from coaches and teammates, continuing the cycle of criticism. I was spiraling out of control.

I made it through three days of this humiliating and self-destructing behavior. I walked into the coach's office and told him it just wasn't working. He quickly agreed and graciously gave me an opportunity to save face by inviting me to come back after my planned two-year volunteer church mission if I wanted to try again. I walked away from my dreams of playing football and entered the sauna of self-pity. I had quit. I did what many others have done and will continue to do when life knocks them down and becomes tough. I stayed down. I failed to prepare for the adversity I would face when I came to Ricks College.

As soon as I walked out of the head coach's office, I knew I had done the wrong thing. I was so embarrassed with myself and the choice I had made. I felt like a loser. No, I was a loser. I had quit. As embarrassing and humiliating as that decision was, it taught me another valuable lesson about the desire of your dreams. The lesson I learned was simply this: Quitters never win while winners never quit. Quitting only leads one way and that way is to failure. However, to fail, fall, or stumble does not mean we have to quit. It gives us another opportunity to get back up and choose again to move forward. The daily choices we make when we fail are simple. First, we can either stay down and give up forever, or we can get back up and succeed. The difference in reaching our dream is the desire we have to make the right choice all the time. It's possible.

Looking back on that day, I realize if you don't have a genuine desire or you lack clear vision of your dream, you will quit. I truly didn't have either. I do believe I lacked the vision more than the desire to play college football at that time. I also learned when you come to that metaphoric fork in the road and have to make any decision in life, either good or bad, the subsequent choices that follow will usually compound the situation both good or bad. The consequences or rewards from these choices continue to get bigger and bigger as you continue down the path you pick. This is one of the reasons why it is so important to prepare to make the right choices from the beginning. Be mindful of your dreams and make sure your desires are genuine. Genuine desires help us prepare. We can always look back and see what we did wrong or what we could have done better, but we need to focus our attention on what is ahead. This preparation for future situations is known as foresight. Foresight can eliminate embarrassment and failure. It can give us 20/20 vision to fulfill our genuine desires. Unfortunately for me, I didn't have foresight.

Walking into the office and telling my coach I was quitting was easy compared to what happened next. The memory still haunts me to this day, and is still very shameful for me. I picked up the phone and called my parents to tell them the bad news.

"Dad...um...Mom...um...I have some bad news."

"What is it son," they asked simultaneously, one on the upstairs phone and the other on the downstairs one.

"The coaches just cut me from the team."

The silence on the other line was palpable. I lied to them. I'm sure my parents knew something wasn't right but they continued to listen to my lies and excuses. I was convinced I couldn't tell them the truth because my dad and mom didn't raise me to quit and I didn't want to disappoint them. They didn't raise me to lie either. My conflicting desires got the best of me that day. I was unprepared for the adversity, I couldn't handle the criticism, and I didn't have a clear vision. It was obvious I had lost this battle, but fortunately for me the war wasn't over. My parents also taught me that when, and not if, life ever knocks you down you get back up and try again. That's exactly what I did.

That's exactly what I invite you to do too. Try again. Take a look at your Dream Bucket list and put your dreams in order of importance. Do you have any conflicting desires? Are your desires sincere? Are your desires burning? Are your desires definite? Every day after you wake up and before you go to bed I want you to look at your list and envision yourself doing them, having them, or even being them. It's possible!

Definite Desire
www.griffinmotivation.com/definitedesire

Jeff Griffin anticipating the next play.

MILE MARKER 3

Second Chances

Mile Marker 3–Second Chances

I walked away from football but I wasn't going to walk away from my other childhood dream: to serve a two-year proselyting mission for my church, the Church of Jesus Christ of Latter-Day Saints. After one semester of college classes, the time had come for me to leave.

My mission call arrived in the mail. The feelings I felt when I opened my recruitment letter from BYU were very similar to the ones I experienced then. I was called to serve and labor among the people of Barcelona, Spain. I was both excited and nervous. I had never been outside the United States besides British Columbia, Canada, and Tijuana, Mexico. Both cities border the United States and really don't count as an "outside the country" experience in my mind.

It may not have been the football field, but it was the mission field and I was given a second chance to lead and play on the mission team. Even though I had never flown before I was put in charge as the travel leader. My assignment was to make sure that 10 other missionaries, including myself, made it from Salt Lake City to the Spanish consulate in Los Angeles before flying to Spain. I found the transport van, picked up our visas at the Spanish consulate, and made it back to airport in time for our flight to Spain.

I learned a lot about myself during those two days of traveling and being travel leader. I realized I could do hard things, that others could rely on me and count on me to follow through with an assignment or task, and I could succeed, even if it was my first time doing it. That experience, though small, was a success nonetheless. It led to other small successes that in return led to bigger and greater successes. It really was as simple as taking one step after the next.

The next two years of serving and working with the people of Spain taught me a lot about myself. I learned what I was capable of doing and what I could become. I learned what it meant to prepare and perform. I also learned a little bit more about success and what is required to achieve it. I learned how to set realistic and reasonable goals. My true desires naturally became more real as my vision increased by seeing the big picture and experiencing life a little more. I had the opportunity to practice the law of attraction and start becoming the person I wanted to be around. I had the opportunity to work hard and keep going even when it seemed hopeless. It was the hardest two years of my life. However, these were also the best two years of experience to prepare me for the best years of my life. It was an experience I wouldn't trade for a million dollars.

My two years of service in Spain taught me discipline. My mission taught me how to deal with failure and how to avoid the poor choices that precede it. It taught me how to plan and prepare. It taught me how to perservere and to keep going forward. It taught me how to look for the good when everything around me was completely bleak. It taught me to enjoy the journey and experience the moment and not just strive for the destination. It taught me how to believe in myself when nobody else did. It taught me that without hope I had nothing. It taught me how to deal with adversity. It even taught me that everyone deserves a second chance, everyone. Even me.

Ruben Gonzalez, a three-time Olympian once said that nine out of ten people quit at anything they do. If this is true, there are nine unsuccessful people for every one successful person. Those aren't very good odds. In fact, they're depressing and almost intimidating. The idea that only one-tenth of people succeed is harsh. I know; I was one of them. I'd like to change that statistic and say that ten out of ten people quit sometime in their life. I've learned no one is perfect. Not even the one out of ten. If we are completely honest with ourselves, we can find a time in our lives when we have given up and quit. We all deserve a second chance. We all need someone to pick us up and show us the way.

Look at Abraham Lincoln. He campaigned for several political races throughout his life and didn't win them all. In fact, he lost the majority of them. He was the underdog for the Republican Party nomination in 1860 behind four other worthy competitors. He didn't quit and never lost hope. He might have lost some battles but he didn't lose the war. Abraham Lincoln understood this concept of getting back up and trying again after you fall, fail, or quit. A person who falls and gets back up is stronger than one who never falls in the first place.

Thomas Edison also learned this lesson. He didn't discover the lightbulb in 1879 on his first try. It is written in *Think and Grow Rich* that Thomas Edison failed more than 10,000 times before getting it right. What was the difference? The difference between him and others was his ability to keep on going without giving up. Each time he got it wrong he picked himself up and kept on going until he got it right. Who do you suppose stumbles and falls more–a person who is successful or one who is a failure? They both stumble and fall but the person who stumbles and falls the most is the one who succeeds. Both are guaranteed to fall and stumble. The major difference between them is the person who succeeds will always get up at least one more time. Thomas Edison didn't succeed until after failing 10,000 times, but he got back up and did it.

Christopher Columbus is another example of someone who picked himself up one more time and didn't give up. He could have listened to the "boo-birds" of his time. He had been described as a failed administrator and naive entrepreneur. He was told what he dreamed about doing was impossible. Today, what is impossible is to disagree that he was one of the greatest mariners in history, a visionary genius, and a national hero. There is no question Christopher Columbus had some setbacks and challenges to overcome, but he didn't quit when adversity intensified. Christopher Columbus refused to give in to discouragement and instead developed a true desire. He had established a clear vision of what he wanted and believed he could achieve it. He then set out and accomplished it.

All these men failed at one time or another just like everybody else had failed before. But every one of these great men succeeded because they got back up one more time. The truth is, we can all succeed. The trick is knowing how to do it and having the courage to make some changes to accomplish it. In other words, establishing a truer desire and a clearer vision will give us the strength to accomplish our dreams. A clear concentrated focus on what we really want will help us drown out the naysayers in the world and set in motion our will to win.

By the end of my mission I was a completely different person than when I started. I was ready to get back home. I was ready to get back to school. I was ready to play some football. I wrote a letter to my coaches letting them know I was ready to give it a second chance if they would allow me to come back and compete for a starting position. I wanted a jersey and I wanted to play. I was ready to succeed and I wanted to win. I was ready to fulfill my dream. I had a true desire and I was prepared this time. The vision was brighter, the expectations were clearer, and I knew what was required to compete at the next level. I understood the road of opposition and adversity much better. When it presented itself again I would be ready.

I made it back to campus just in time for the winter

semester. Conditioning for the upcoming season had just gotten started. I had less than seven months to get back into shape. No problem, I had a plan! My first goal was to be faster than before. I wanted to at least be as fast as Hall-of-Famer Steve Largent of the Seattle Seahawks, and run the 40-yard dash in 4.6 seconds or less. My second goal was to ignore the negative voices and focus on the positive ones. Instead of worrying about dropping the ball, I was going to focus on catching the ball. My last goal was to believe in myself and know that I was a winner. I didn't want too many goals to focus on because I learned if you have too many goals you aren't very effective with any of them. Having too many goals dilutes the power of focus. It dilutes your ability to improve and to overcome. When I try to catch more than one ball at a time I end up dropping both of them, leaving me empty-handed.

Seven months of conditioning is a very short time to get back into shape. I thought I would be okay getting back into shape with all the walking I did in Spain during the past two years. I believed my legs would be ready for the rigors of plyometric conditioning. My first day back to the gym was difficult but rewarding. I had started seven stations and I had finished seven stations without major embarrassment or damage to my body. I left the gym exhausted and surprisingly full of energy. My mind and body were invigorated as I cleaned up in the locker room. I ate, did my homework, and went to bed feeling great.

When I woke up the next morning I couldn't move or get out of bed. My legs wouldn't move and my body had developed rigor mortis during the night. I finally got my legs off the bed but couldn't seem to get them to lift me up. After a few minutes of sitting on the side of my bed contemplating how I was going to get to the bathroom in time I simply willed my muscles to move. I rose from the bed and made it to the bathroom. Once on my feet and moving again, I was fine. The trick was sitting down and getting back up. There was a certain point, as I sat down at my desk or any other seat, when my muscles would give out and I would just have to plop down into the seat. Walking up stairs was painful as well. I didn't know how I was going to go through another day of plyometrics. But this time I had chosen and decided before the aches and pains and other troubles ever came that I wasn't going to quit. I was soon amazed at how fast my body warmed up once it got going.

I eventually stopped hurting and began to see the benefits of hard work. Seven months went by faster than I expected and the first day of practice was upon us. As always, opposition arrived and my first bout with trouble presented itself as a major head cold. I couldn't breathe and I ached all over. I kept telling myself, "Big deal. Who cares? I don't! It's mind over matter. If you don't mind, then it really doesn't matter.

I wasn't going to let a little adversity get me down, not this time. I had planned for it and I was ready for whatever came my way. Even if I wasn't completely prepared for it I knew it would pass and I would get through it the best I could.

The first day of practice was always the time trials. The coaches and staff measure your vertical jump, your 40-yard dash, and the dreaded "Viking Challenge" (VC).[2]

My cold was getting worse but I couldn't quit now. I had to see if I measured up, especially to myself. I had to know if I

[2]The VC is where you start at one end of the football field on the goal line. The whistle blows and you sprint to the 10-yard line and run back to where you started. Without stopping, you sprint back to the 25-yard line and return again to the beginning. Still sprinting at full speed, you run to the 50-yard line and back. Your body begs you to stop. Your heart is pumping twice as fast as it was in the beginning. Your lungs are about to burst from lack of oxygen. Your body is screaming. This is when you must remind yourself this is only temporary. Although you know you're almost finished, you clearly understand there is another set of sprints looming ahead. They are the hardest ones left–the 75- and 100-yard sprints. In between these longer yards of sprinting you attempt to

had improved physically and I had to know I would accomplish my goals. I had to overcome and not quit, not this time.

I started with the 40-yard dash. I was hoping it would be good. There was no more preparing at this point. The moment of preparation had passed and the moment of performance had arrived. I approached the starting line with two other receivers. "The last time I did this, I was blown out of the water," I thought to myself. With a more positive attitude I thought, "This time will be different."

The gun went off, the coaches started their stopwatches, and we shot off the line. Racing down the track with the wind in my hair, I glanced over from the corner of my eye to the right and then to the left while never slowing down. I was doing it! I was maintaining my speed. In fact, I was slightly ahead of one of the other receivers. Almost simultaneously, all three of us crossed the finish line. On cue the coaches stopped their watches. I went over to the coach in charge of my time and hesitantly asked for my time.

"Griffin, your time is…4.7 seconds!"

It wasn't the 4.6 or less goal I set earlier in the year but it wasn't the 5.1 I ran two years earlier. Having a head cold, I could accept it with honor and chalk it up as my first small step of success. I had improved. I still had to be faster for next year but for now I was pleased. I went over to the team manager and gave him my time so it could be recorded.

"One event down, two more to go," I thought as I walked off to the next test. The vertical jump was next. I increased my

---

mentally find a happy place in the back of your mind to alleviate the searing pain. Nearing the goal line, you come out of the foggy numbness and you touch the starting line. You begin to doubt and flirt with the idea of quitting as you turn around and continue down the field to the 75-yard line. On the way back to the starting line you pass other participants who look like you feel. Running by yourself you silently wonder if this is really what you signed up for. Touching the goal line for the last time you turn around to make the final sprint, knowing this is exactly what you signed up for. The last 100 is the fastest and the longest. You give it everything you've got, knowing the VC is the last thing you have to do for the day. Every player dreads the Viking Challenge.

vertical by 4 inches. That felt nice. The dreaded VC was all I had left. That too went well, considering the circumstances. The season was off to a great start.

After the first week of practice the coaches assigned everybody to their roles and assignments. The coaches assigned each player a spot on the team. The three spots an offensive player could be assigned to were first team offense, second team offense, or the "scrub" team offense. Regrettably for me, I was assigned to the scrub team. I didn't let it bother me. It didn't matter that much because I wasn't going to stay there forever.

I wasn't going to let anything get me down. It's easier to quit if you let adversity get you down. Also, you can't perform at your best if you're dwelling on the negative. Negative energy will always take away from positive energy. This year I was determined to look for the positive even when things looked bad.

Being on the scrub team is not the first team offense but it did have its perks. One of the perks was that we got to practice against the first team defense every day. We played against the best defense in the whole conference. In fact, it was the best defense in the entire country. At the end of the 1994 season our team ended up ranked second in the country with a perfect 11-0 record. We were very successful that year. By playing against the first team defense every day I was positive my personal offensive skills would improve immensely, even to the point where I would move up and eventually play for the first team squad.

Most practices were the same. We would come out, compete, and get beat up. Some of us nicknamed our team the "meat squad" because we would come off the field battered and bruised. However, on other days the meat squad shined.

These days were special. It was as if nothing could go wrong and everything went right. Scoring on the first team defense was the best. After running a great route, catching the ball, and making a move on them to score a touchdown, I would come back to the line of scrimmage with greater determination to be even better the next time.

I would also have a little fun with the defense. On my way back to the huddle I would toss them the ball as I jogged past and jokingly say, "Nice defense." Without fail they would throw the ball at me. The ball would sail past my head, missing me either on the right or on the left but missing me completely almost every time. Without stopping I would turn around and shout back with a smile, "That's why you play defense!" This kind of friendly trash talking would get me into trouble the very next play but I didn't care, I was having fun. I was working hard and finding pleasure with the small successes I had while playing on the scrub team. Although pleasurable and fun, the scrub team wasn't what I was striving for. This wasn't the dream I had envisioned.

On home games the coaches would let everybody dress, including the scrub players. I guess they wanted more cheerleaders on the sideline because everyone knew we weren't getting any playing time. We wouldn't get to play even if one of the first stringers got hurt or injured. There were always the second and third stringers to replace them. It didn't matter to me though, I was enjoying the moment. The sounds, the smells, and the sights I experienced during games were amazing. It was still great being on the sideline listening to the pads popping with every great hit. It was fun listening to the chatter going back and forth between opponents. It was great to experience the whole game as close as anyone could without actually playing. The only way I was getting in at this point was to hope for a blowout. Everyone who has ever played sports knows the only time scrub players get any playing time is when you're either killing the opponent or getting killed yourselves.

That time came against the University of New Mexico Academy where I got to experience what it would be like to be part of the first team and play! Two plays were all I got during the 1994 football season. Two plays were all I needed to give me a taste of what it could be. Two plays were enough to make up for all the hard work I put into all those practices up until that moment. Two plays were all it took to solidify my desires, clarify my dreams, and recommit to work even harder. I knew I was on the right road to accomplishing them.

The team ended the season with a bowl victory and a perfect record. We were ranked second in the nation and because of our success we had many players leave the team and go on to bigger ones. They were offered division 1 (D1) scholarships to many of the top programs in the nation. Some went to Stanford. Others went to University of Utah. Most went on to BYU where I was hoping to follow someday.

I made a goal for the following season to fill in one of the empty spots. I believed one of those positions belonged to me. I needed to use the rest of the year and the following summer to get bigger, faster, and stronger. I was going to contribute next year. I was going to compete for one of those positions and I was going to obtain it. I had a goal and I was going to succeed.

Now that your Dream Bucket list is filled out and your Desires have been examined and nurtured, I invite you to make a plan and tackle your dreams one at a time. I want you to DO IT. I know you can DO IT! Begin again, and again, and again if you need to, but DO them! Live them! Achieve them! Make a plan for your goal. Write down your progress and keep track of your successes. If you succeed in planning, then you can plan on succeeding. You're possible!

Gooooaaal

Go to www.griffinmotivation.com/goals and download a worksheet to assist you with this step.

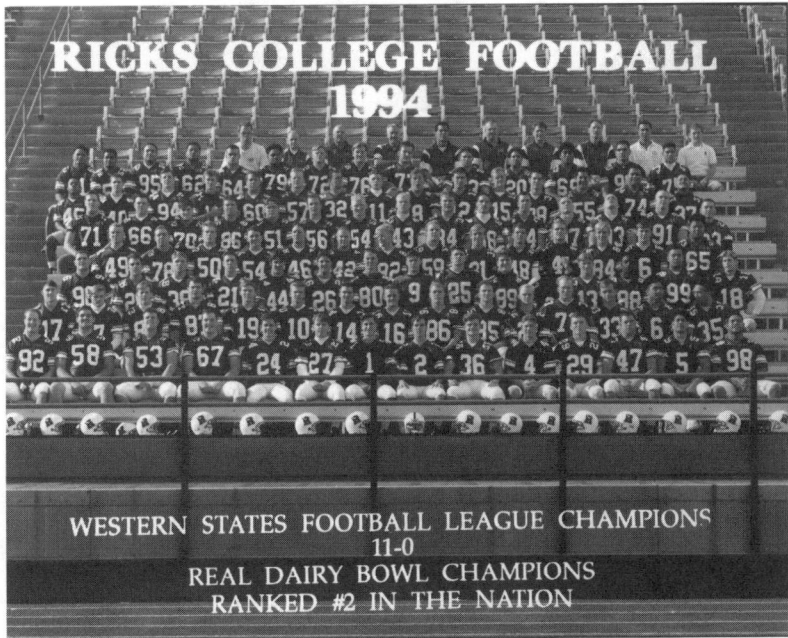

Member of the team. The Ricks College Vikings had a perfect season, 11-0.

MILE MARKER 4

Good in All
Things

Mile Marker 4—Good in All Things

"Jeff…Jeff…" I started to return from the recesses of my mind as I heard Doug's voice.

"…Jeff!" Doug's voice brought me back to reality.

"They don't have 9-1-1 here!"

"You're kidding me, right?" I dubiously asked.

"No, I'm not. They don't have 9-1-1, but I called the ambulance and they're on their way."

We could hear the insects flying overhead and wind blowing through the leaves of the trees as we both paused and let reality sink in. I finally broke the silence with a simple question.

"Doug, will you do me a favor," I asked.

"Yeah sure, anything," he quickly responded.

"Will you give me a blessing?" In our religion, we believe righteous men who hold the priesthood of God can anoint the sick with consecrated oil and give blessings of faith and healing by laying their hands on the head of the one requesting the blessing.

My mother was the one who taught me how to pray. I always drew strength from her, especially during difficult times. She taught me faith-filled stories my whole life. She took most of them from the Bible. Some of my favorites came from the Old Testament. There's the story of Abraham that taught me how I too can have great love for both God and family but choosing God over everything and everyone is the greatest choice one can make. The story of Joseph taught me how I too must simply forgive my brothers when they come begging for help during good times and hard times. I often used the story of David to find courage when I had to go up against my own Goliaths. The story of Elijah and the dying widow taught me how I must practice my faith in the prophet's words and trust them even if it looks like I will die trying. I love the story about Daniel and his three friends who stood firm in their knowledge of eating healthy food and praying daily to their God while the king insisted they eat his food and pray to his gods.

Although these stories are inspiring and interesting, the stories that came to my mind as I laid on the ground were the ones found in the four gospels of the New Testament. I truly believe the miracles that happened in the New Testament continue to happen today. I've seen them firsthand as my family and I have lived the teachings of Jesus Christ. I've personally witnessed many of the same miracles that took place during the ministry of the Savior's life. They happened when others, including myself, followed the simple formula of having faith in God and believing that His power can touch and heal every aspect of our lives if we but follow and obey Him. I truly believe all things are possible when we invite the Creator of this world into our lives. One way to invite Him is through prayer.

"Absolutely," Doug responded with courage. "Do you have any oil?"

"No," I said, while hoping he had some instead. "Do you?"

"No."

"Don't we make a pair," I thought. "We're the most unprepared returned missionaries out there." I reminded Doug of our other option, which was to go ask our client if she had any. He took off to the house, once again leaving me alone with my thoughts.

"I do believe in God," I thought. "I know He cares about me, but this was my own fault. I got myself into this mess. I was the one who set up the scaffolding wrong. Will He really listen to me now?" Before the darkness and doubt could completely enter my mind Doug came running out the door, lifted something in the air, and shouted, "I've got it!" He jumped off the porch, sprinted across the lawn, and ran over to where I was lying. He stopped short of where I was and knelt down next to me. I could see his courage had wavered a little bit, but it didn't matter anymore. At least I had someone there by my side.

I looked up while Doug was trying to open the little vial of olive oil. He was visibly shaking. He finally got the lid off and attempted to put a single drop on my head. It didn't go as planned. Instead of a single drop, several came out because his hands were shaking with adrenalin. I felt like a Caesar salad. Doug replaced the cap set it on the ground. He placed his hands my head and began praying for me. The shakiness of his hands began to slow down and the quiver in his voice started to subside. I remember feeling an unmistakable calmness come over us when he said that all would be fine and I would recover from this accident. I wanted to believe, I really did. But there was another little piece of me that still doubted. After concluding the blessing, I thanked Doug. He looked back down at me and shrugged his shoulders and said, "You're lucky we're outside because if we weren't, I don't think my prayer would have made it past the ceiling."

"Doug, you did fine," I responded earnestly.

Still not believing he did a good job, I continued to let Doug know he did great, despite his shaky hands and quivery voice. It wasn't until months later and several reassurances from me that Doug finally believed he did a good job. Time is a wonderful elixir. We joke about that experience to this day. As time goes by it becomes more and more humorous.

The truth is, you can honestly find good things to focus on even during the most difficult times of your life. Hindsight is 20/20. Everything becomes more clear looking back. The key to life is working on 20/20 *foresight*. We must prepare the

51

best we can for those difficult times that do come and will continue to come. Ever since that fateful summer at Ricks College when I quit the team I have tried to live by that invaluable lesson learned: Prepare for anything. "If you fail to prepare, then prepare to fail." I realize some may be concerned or overwhelmed by the idea of preparing for everything. I understand life, school, work, and even play can be cruel for whatever reason.

We don't always know what problems will come our way. Unfortunately, we, ourselves, are the cause of most of our own mistakes and problems in life. That is why we need to establish a solid foundation of true principles, truths that are and were and will always be for anyone and everyone. (For more information on these truths look for my book: *I'Mpossible: 5 Keystone Habits Highly Successful Leaders Persist In*) Then we can base our choices around them to minimize our problems and errors. Nobody is perfect! We all make mistakes—some more than others. One of the steps to success is to minimize those mistakes. We can learn from our own mistakes or from the mistakes of others. When we don't quit and look for the good in all things, whether we are fast learners or not, we can succeed. Our capacity to gain knowledge and truth is essential for minimizing our mistakes and maximizing our chances for success.

I could hear the sirens from the ambulance. It was racing down the road leaving a wake of dust in its tracks. It turned in to where we were and came to a screeching halt, causing the dust to swirl out and up from under the tires. The first EMT jumped out of the ambulance and ran over to myside to begin taking my vital signs.

"You're alive!" one of the EMTs exclaimed. I wasn't quite sure how to handle that comment. "Good to know," I thought.

"I'm glad you pointed out the obvious." I sarcastically thought, "Now I'll be able to relax a little easier, knowing that I'm alive." I wasn't sure if they were telling me I was alive because I was, or if they were trying to take my mind away from the fact I had just damaged my body to the point I probably wouldn't walk again, let alone play football. Truth be known, it was kind of funny that they told me I was alive while I was conscious. I chuckled a little but it didn't really matter what they said at that point; I just wanted the pain to go away. I was surprised at how much pain was shooting through my body, especially in my legs.

When they rolled me on the board, tied me down to the gurney, and lifted me into the ambulance, I had to check, double check, and triple check to make sure they hadn't folded my legs underneath me. It felt like they folded me in half like a rag doll, with my feet resting by my ears. The pulling sensation on the upper part of my thighs was intense. It was as if I had just finished a major leg workout at the gym followed by a quick rest on the bed with your legs hanging over the edge to give the taut muscles in your thighs an opportunity to stretch, but a hundred times worse.

As they were closing the doors I implored, "Can I have some drugs for the pain?"

"Sorry, we have to get you to the doctors first."

"Okay then, let's go."

That was it for now. No need to complain about what I couldn't have. Complaining about spilled milk was never an option in my family. This reminded me of a saying I committed to memory as a teenager:

"For every worry under the sun, there is a solution or there is none. If there be one hurry and find it, if there be none never mind it."

The ambulance sped off to the hospital with its precious

cargo locked down inside it. The workers there called it a hospital but it really was more like a small clinic. Once we arrived, they pulled me out of the ambulance and rushed me into the emergency room. The pain in my body was increasing every minute. As they raced me into the clinic I saw some new faces so I decided to ask again. "Can I have some drugs?"

They answered with precision, "No sir. Not yet."

"Why so mean," I wondered.

"We have to take a picture of your body before we can give you any drugs," they quickly explained before walking away. I held on to that comment knowing as soon as the picture was taken, I was going to get some relief from this tremendous pain. I closed my eyes and patiently waited for the doctor to come.

I was startled by a sound by my side and quickly opened my eyes. It was a nurse who came in, leaned down, and softly spoke to me as a concerned human being. She asked if I wanted a blessing. She too believed in the power and energy from above that enters our body, spirit, and mind if we allow it to.

"No thank you," I kindly declined. "My buddy already gave me one."

I believe in God and I believe there really is an unseen power we can connect to. Some call this source the supreme power, great spirit, Allah, Buddha, etc. I like to address Him as Heavenly Father. This power or energy can improve our situation, surroundings, and life. We always hear about the spirit of winning, the spirit of giving, the spirit of intention, etc. The bottom line is there is a spirit within us that wants to be connected with its source whether we consciously choose to connect with it or not. If we do, we will have added strength that makes the difference between a good thing happening and a great thing happening.

I thought her question was sincere and heartfelt. It was good to see professionals in the medical field who have spent their careers studying how best to care for, comfort, and cure the physically sick and afflicted individuals who come into their facilities with modern medicines, also understanding that there is more to healing than just a pill or a prescription. I appreciated her recognizing there is more to us than just our physical bodies and our physical bodies are just the outer shell that encases our inner selves.

The main doctor on call finally approached me and told me the bad news. The equipment they had in their clinic was not sufficient to get a clear picture of my back. "We're going to send you to Ogden," he said.

"Can I have some drugs then," I asked, knowing it was a two-hour ride from Preston to Ogden.

"No. We want you to be able to tell the doctors where it hurts."

I couldn't believe what I was hearing. I wanted to reach up and slap him on both sides of the cheeks and say, "Are you kidding me? It hurts everywhere. Just give me something to help the pain, anything!" That thought brought a smile to my face but I continued to plead with the doctor, "Can I at least have the helicopter ride?"

"No," the doctor answered again. "By the time the helicopter gets here, picks you up, and takes you back, the ambulance will have gotten you there at about the same time for a whole lot less."

"Can I at least have some Tylenol," I pleaded. The answer was still the same,

"No."

I was dejected.

With the new order given, I was quickly put back on the

gurney and rushed back off to the awaiting ambulance. As I was being reloaded into the ambulance I recognized I had two new EMTs. "Maybe they will help me out," I thought. As we got on our way I asked them, "Would one of you do me a favor?"

"Yeah, sure! What is it," they helpfully replied.

"Can one of you give me some drugs?"

They looked at each other before squirming around a bit and said, "Sorry bud, doctor's orders."

I had to try!

The fastest way from Preston to Ogden is through Logan. But if you recall, there was road construction blocking that route. The only alternative was the back roads. If you've ever seen the movie *Napoleon Dynamite*, you'll know Preston is farm country. Farm country is loaded with dirt roads. Dirt roads are loaded with pot holes and rocks. Every hole, every rock, and every pebble the ambulance ran over vibrated its way up through the tires, past the shocks, and straight to my injured back.

It reminded me of the story of the princess and the pea. This is the fairytale about the peasant girl who was asked to sleep on a pile of mattresses to determine whether or not she was a suitable match for the prince. But instead of sleeping through the night, she tossed and turned because of an unknown single pea that was placed at the bottom of the pile of mattresses. The princess felt the pea and I was feeling the pebbles. The stories aren't the same but the titles are very similar. My story would be called the painter and the pebble.

Each time the ambulance ran over a rock or into a pot hole it sent indescribable pain throughout my body. The driver was swerving all over the road trying to do his best to avoid the worst of the pot holes. I know those were his intentions, but for a split second my cynic mind convinced me the navigator, or copilot of the ambulance, was pointing out the biggest and worst bumps in the road. Once identified, the driver would quickly comply by cranking the steering wheel to one side, maneuvering the ambulance across the road to the other side, and hitting the bumps at full speed. As fast as the thought came, it left. However, the rough ride continued. It became so bumpy at times that even though I was tied down and secured, I would glance down at my legs to see if they had bounced off the gurney and were hanging off the bed.

It was the longest three hours of my life. I'm sure it was for the EMTs as well. I was like that annoying little brother or sister on vacation who asks every five minutes, "Are we there yet?" "How much longer?" "I'm bored!" "Are we there yet?" The closer we got to the hospital the more the pain intensified. My journey had just begun and I had many more miles to go. I needed to do something to get rid of the pain, but what?

I remembered the time my buddy saw a birthing moving in school. He passed out and lost consciousness because of the sight of blood. Another buddy of mine cut his finger and because of the sight of blood and the intense pain he too passed out. I was experiencing a lot of pain but apparently it wasn't enough to lose consciousness. I also wasn't losing or seeing any blood so what was my next option? I inhaled deeply, clenched my fists, and held my breath. My buddies and I purposely helped each other pass out when we were younger. We would hyperventilate with our heads between our legs and stand up as fast as we could, holding our breath, while someone pressed down on our chest. I wouldn't recommend this to anyone but it worked every time. I proceeded to hold my breath.

"What are you doing," the EMTs asked, looking down at

me with expressions of wonder and confusion.

I exhaled noisily and said, "Nothing, it's not working."

My next thought was to ask one of the EMTs to hit me as hard as they could in the middle of my forehead. While boxing with my friends as a teenager, I learned quickly you could get knocked out if you struck your opponent hard enough on the forehead. Looking up at the EMTs, I implored both of them, "Will one of you two do me a favor?" Knowing what my last request was, they were reluctant to answer.

"Sure, what is it?"

"Will one of you hit me..." pointing to my forehead, "as hard as you can right here?"

They looked at each other, smiled, shook their heads and said, "Sorry bud, doctor's orders."

I rolled my eyes and shook my head while we all had a quick laugh. Still a little dejected about not being able to lose consciousness or get the EMTs to help me pass out, I thought, "I still need to do something to get my mind off this pain." The answer came instantly, "Tell some jokes!"

I started to tell them the joke about a man traveling to Timbuktu. When I got halfway through my joke, one EMT looked at the other and said, "Do you want to hit him or do you want me to?" I thought it was a good joke. They did too but they wanted to have a little fun in a bad situation. It worked. We laughed, exchanged jokes, and focused on the positive. That day I found Peace in the pain. We eventually made it to Ogden with smiles on our faces.

There is darkness and discouragement all around us. There is goodness and light as well. It just depends on which one we want to focus on. Today I invite you to look for the good in all things and thank God you get to experience it. One way I remind myself to be positive when times get tough and I forget to see the good is I reach down to my wrist and pull on my "I'Mpossible" reminder band and let it snap me back to my dreams. If yours has broken or you would like another one, go to the link below and get one for both you and your friends.

I'Mpossible Band
www.griffinmotivation.com/bracelet

A simple tool to amplify your power and potential. Go to www.griffinmotivation.com to flip the switch.

MILE MARKER 5

Rebuild & Renew

Mile Marker 5—Rebuild and Renew

We finally arrived at McKay Dee hospital in Ogden, Utah. I had never been so excited to get to a hospital in my life. I wanted out of the ambulance and into the open arms of professional caregivers. I wanted relief from the pain. I wanted to know for certain what exactly had happened to my back.

The ambulance pulled up and stopped next to the automatic sliding doors of the emergency room. The EMTs opened the back doors and jumped out on cue. Light rushed in and fresh new air replaced the old. They pulled me out of the ambulance once again and rushed me into the emergency room.

This was a happening place! It was a lot busier than the last hospital. Nurses and technicians were moving at a pace like they were running on undiluted caffeine. Doctors were working with purpose. I thought I had just entered the emergency beltway. I wouldn't have been surprised to run across an emergency traffic cop in the room. I knew immediately I would be able to get some treatment here.

I began asking anyone who walked past my gurney if I could have some drugs. "Drugs, can I have some drugs," I blurted out to the nurse carrying saline solution to an awaiting patient. She barely flinched as she looked down at me while never breaking stride. Another nurse was approaching, but he too looked like he had something else to do and somewhere else to go. "Hey, you," lifting an arm and pointing to the oncoming nurse, "can I have some drugs?" The same result occurred with the third and fourth as well. After what seemed like an eternity, it appeared an attendee was coming my way. Without waiting for him to ask any questions or say hello I

61

simply asked one more time, "Can I have some drugs?"

Instantly, they started putting needles and tubes in places I never believed needles and tubes could go. "Oh… they can put that there," I wondered without shock or disgust. Before doing anything else like taking x-rays or diagnosing the problem, the medical personnel injected some type of medicine into my IV. I could literally feel it enter my bloodstream. It felt warm and comforting like my childhood blanket. The relief was instantaneous. It only took the edge off a fraction of the pain but it was still such a relief.

I needed more! I wanted more. "More!" was my simple command. They complied without hesitating and gave me more. Again, as the medicine entered my body the level of pain dropped just a fraction. I was two for two on my requests at this point so I went for request number three. "More…!" I pleaded with the best puppy dog eyes impression I could do. I was surprised by the response and elated at the same time. They inserted the syringe in the IV a third time and gave me more of the blessed pain medication. By this time the pain was all but gone and I was feeling a whole lot better. My feet and legs felt soft and light like they were starting to float. I was feeling more comfortable than I had on the bumpy ride down here. This feeling was addictive and so I asked for a fourth dosage. "M-O-R-E?" was all I could get out.

"No more," the attendee quickly responded. "Doctor's orders." I rolled my eyes and grinned, thinking it never hurts to ask. You'll always miss 100 percent of the shots you don't take. I was taking my shots.

Now that the pain was manageable, the "experts" were ready to do their job. They rolled me into a dark secluded room where a huge machine was waiting. The x-ray machine looked like a giant metal altar just waiting to sacrifice its next victim.

I was that victim. The nurses, combined with help from the doctor, lifted me off the gurney and transferred me over to the flat surface of the x-ray bed. Lying there on my back waiting for the picture to be taken with nothing to do or nowhere to go, my attention was diverted to the chilly touch of the machine. The cold stainless-steel table began to seep through my tattered shirt and enter through my skin. The change of temperature felt good to my body. Everyone left the room except for the technician. Eventually the technician left as well, leaving me all alone. The solitude of being by myself gave me a glimpse of the difficulty and darkness that lay ahead of me. It left me somewhat awestruck and a little bit scared. I didn't know what to expect. With that said, I still wouldn't allow the fear to control my thoughts and attitude.

The x-ray was taken and the results were sent to the doctor in charge. I was returned to a waiting area where I contemplated the future. Time alone while you are waiting for serious news can do a number on your psyche, both good and bad. I was starting to let negative thoughts enter my mind when the curtains slid back and in walked my mom and dad. Instantly, any negative thoughts I had earlier, vanished. My support system had arrived–spiritually, socially, morally, mentally, physically, and financially. They have always been there for me, they would always be there for me, and most importantly, they were now there to support me in the most trying time of my life.

As I saw them enter my room a smile broke out and stretched across my face. I was so glad to see them. I'm not quite sure they were as glad to see me. I was lying there with my clothes cut off, tubes sticking out of my body, and blood oozing from my flesh wounds. Mom appeared strong and didn't cry. During a crisis, my mom is a rock. She supports, loves, and asks the right questions while she's around you but later, when she is alone, she cries and relives the whole thing. Dad was standing there silently with his arms crossed. He didn't want his emotions to betray him but the quiet confidence, love, and hope he had for his son could be felt by all, especially from me.

The doctor came in with the results. The look on his face said it all. "Jeff," he began, "your L-1 (Lumbar) vertebrae has been shattered." He continued as a professional should. "It exploded from the force of the fall, damaging your spinal cord." Without letting any of us respond, he finished with the diagnosis. "Your T-12 (Thoracic) vertebrae is compressed as well."

The silence in the room was palpable. The hum of the air vent was drowning out the noise in my head. You could almost hear everybody's heart beating out of their chest. Each word from the doctor was like a blow from a heavyweight boxer. The knockout punch came next.

"You're paralyzed from the waist down..." The room began to circle and I almost didn't hear what came next.

"You'll neither walk nor move your legs again. We've scheduled a time for your surgery to repair your spine the best we can." The lights were going out and the doctor was almost finished.

"Do you have any questions you would like me to answer?" We sat there in silence, not knowing what else to say or do.

"If you need anything," the doctor continued sympathetically, "let me know. I'll do the best I can to help you."

We said nothing. It felt like the wind had been knocked out of us. The silence was deafening as he looked at us with our mouths half-open. With nothing more to say, the doctor turned and left as fast as he entered.

The news was direct and clear. "Your back is broken." "You are paralyzed from the waist down." "You will never use or move your legs again." Those statements were crystal clear and to the point. I couldn't misinterpret those comments. It was obvious at that moment my dream of playing football at BYU was over. This vicissitude of life had taken my legs and had shattered my childhood dream. I let this realization sink in. I gave it a few minutes to take root. I felt the blow but I felt something else take root as well. It was a certain kind of power that liberated me from the doubt and the fear. This power was mine and it gave me the courage to decide that although this particular dream was over, it didn't mean others couldn't be created.

I had the ability to choose. I still had freewill. I still could dream other dreams. I had a choice. I learned from past experiences that to quit has more damaging effects than moving forward even in times of disappointment and trial. I might have given up and quit in the past, but today I would not let this unfortunate event dictate my attitude and character for the rest of my life. I've learned closed doors in life lead to open windows, and I would wait and watch for what windows would open next.

I spent my first night in the Intensive Care Unit (ICU) under close supervision. My vital signs were all over the place. They were so bad at one particular time that one of the nurses came in, sat down, and held my hand to try to calm me down. My body wasn't used to the foreign objects floating around inside. Shattered vertebrae are not something the body tolerates well. The shock and sudden change was too much for it to handle. It didn't know what to do, but the great caring professionals did. With the help from the ICU nurses, I was able to make it through the night.

During the next two days, a few people were allowed in to see me. Those visits were both uplifting and draining. My spirit would be lifted when they came and my body would be drained as they left. I explained to those who came that my bungee jumping experience planned for the night before came a little earlier than expected. I also joked that I wanted to take up gymnastics since I was so skilled at sticking the landing. With the few visits from loved ones, help from the nurses, and prayers from all, I made it through the next two nights without any complications.

The morning of my scheduled surgery I was rolled into the pre-operation room. Standing above me was my surgeon with his mug of coffee in one hand and a chocolate sprinkled donut in the other. While downing his sugar and caffeine breakfast, he explained again how long the operation would take. He had told my parents and me what he was going to do the day before so I didn't care how long it was going to take, I just wanted it over. At this point, the anesthesiologist came over to inject the medicine into my IV and asked me to count backward from 10. "10…9…8…," was all I got to before I willingly succumbed to the darkness. I can't be 100 percent sure about the exact number but I do know I didn't get to zero. I don't remember anything else after that but 10 hours later I woke up in a different room. The surgery[3] was a success and it went well without any complications.

---

[3]What the doctors did to my body was more like shop class than surgery. They began by making an 18-inch incision across my back. They started from my belly button and went across my torso all the way around to the edge of my backbone. They cut through the muscle and detached my diaphragm. They deflated my left lung and inserted a surgical tube into my side. They pushed the tube in-between my ribs, pulled it out the other side, and inserted it into my lung where it stayed for a couple days. They gathered up all the shattered bone from my back and reused the pieces that were big enough and salvageable. What they weren't able to use, they discarded and used donor bone to replace the missing pieces. They cut the left side of my second-to-last rib completely off. They used the same rib as an added support when they attached a metal plate to my spine. The removed rib sat between my backbone and the metal plate. The plate was 1.5 inches wide by 3 inches long and was

I was wrestling with the blanket of darkness and disorientation that comes from the anesthesia. I was trying to come back to life. My mind wanted to come back to the light but my body was having a hard time doing it. The spirit is willing but the flesh is weak! Finally, both mind and spirit came to a compromise and I came to. I started to stir, groan, and moan. In slurred speech I said, "Pain....I'm...in...pain." I thought I knew what pain was during my ambulance ride to Ogden from Preston, Idaho. I had no clue what real pain felt like. I still probably don't, but I have a better understanding.

Pain medication didn't really work. I went through three different types before finally finding one that worked. I literally couldn't even move a muscle without my body hurting. It took all my energy to just lie there and focus on my breathing. The pain I was experiencing after surgery was so intense. It was the worst so far. At least that's what I thought until the nurses came to finish the "cycle."

The cycle took six hours to fully complete. I didn't do much during those six hours because I couldn't move. The beginning of the cycle started when the nurses rolled me from the left side of the bed to the middle, and then to the other side of the bed every two hours. This was done to prevent bed sores or pressure sores from appearing. Every sixth hour I would dread the sound of approaching footsteps because this is when they would roll me on my left side. My left side was where the

---

fastened by four 1-inch-long screws. They put this plate on the side of my backbone. On the top part of the plate they inserted two of the four screws into the T-12 vertebrae, which was directly above the exploded L-1 vertebrae. They then drilled two more screws into my L-2 vertebrae, on the bottom part of the plate. Now that they had fastened the plate to my vertebrae, my spinal column was more solid and secure than before the accident. The doctors had repaired my broken back but the surgery wasn't finished. Now they had to put me back together again. They inflated my lung, reattached my diaphragm, sewed my muscle back together, and closed me back up by using more than 50 surgical staples. Ten hours later they were finished. It looked like a giant zipper had been inserted in the side of my torso.

staples were. The left side was where the surgical tube was sticking out of my ribs. The left side was where they cut my rib off. The left side was where they deflated my lung. The left side was the source of all the pain. When they rolled me over onto the surgical tube it would send a shock wave of pain through my body that literally took my breath away. Every cycle I wondered, "How bad can bed sores really be?"

I thought I was experiencing the worst possible pain until a few days later when something unexpected happened. I sneezed! The first time I sneezed was also the last time I sneezed for at least six months. Before the sneezing incident I didn't know you could swallow sneezes. I'm a let it out loud and let it land where it may kind of sneezer. I just let sneezes explode from my mouth instead of trying to keep them in and muffled. The sneeze sensation started. I was excited because I always have a sense of relief and satisfaction from a well-orchestrated sneeze. I slowly inhaled and anticipated the explosion of air accompanied with the customary shout-out of "aahh-choo."

I got past the intake of air part of the sneeze when I realized I was in trouble. I always thought you could not stop a sneeze at this point. The beginning of the explosion took place only to fizzle abruptly in the end because of the pain that accompanied this innocent sneeze. Instead of air exploding out my mouth, it felt like my staples had exploded from their place in my side, shooting out with shrapnel, and leaving a wide-open wound. I checked my side, expecting blood to be oozing out. There was nothing but a stapled, closed incision. It was the last time I sneezed that year. I had never experienced pain like that before. I knew after that I was in for a long journey.

During those last couple days and even during my rehabilitation, I experienced excruciating pain. It stemmed from simple everyday movements to major surgery. The pain was so bad I thought I would die, at least I wanted to die a few of those times. I wanted to leave this world if not for a moment, even if it meant being knocked out. It never happened, but I eventually figured out how to substitute the pain with Peace. The peace I found was more exhilarating than the pain. It healed my soul quicker than the medication could heal my body. It gave me courage to fight where the medicine encouraged me to cower. I wasn't instantly made whole nor was the pain completely taken away but I was able to instantly see what would help me be whole.

I spent hours on my back and days wandering the halls in my wheelchair meditating the route I must take to get to the top. I had a lot of time to think and contemplate about the task of rebuilding. This time of recovery gave me an opportunity to meditate about the future and all the endless possibilities ahead. I knew I was going to recover physically, but the real question was would I really ever recover emotionally or mentally? I knew I needed to begin rebuilding my life. I knew more than ever I couldn't do it on my own. I needed to spend more time than just minutes and moments thinking about the Man who could turn the impossible into the possible. I needed to go to Him and plead for help and invite Him to be part of my life.

With the Savior by my side, I was going to overcome and prove the "experts" wrong and walk again. I was going to get back up and sally forth and chart another course. In order to rebuild and recover, I was going to have to fully commit and immerse myself into doing everything humanly possible to accomplish this task. The road to success is paved with the same challenges this road to recovery had and has. I knew I would rebuild and renew my dreams with faith, hope, love, sacrifice, support, work, and perseverance. I AM possible!

Now that you're developing your desire, working on your dreams, filling up your bucket, and looking for the good in all things, I implore you to open a window and ask for help. Ask a friend or a loved one to help you with your journey. Telling someone you completely trust your hopes and dreams and accepting their help will increase your odds for success. Find a positive partner who will support you. I recommend your first partner be God. Start with prayer. We're possible!

Partner with Prayer
www.griffinmotivation.com/prayer

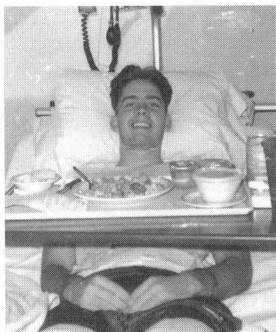

Happy to have a visitor.

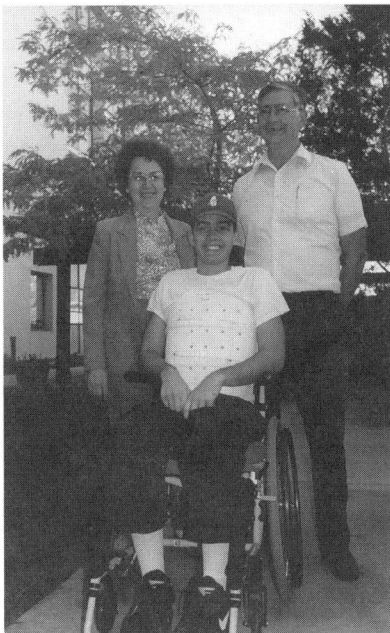

Weekly visit with my parents, Kaylene and Terry.

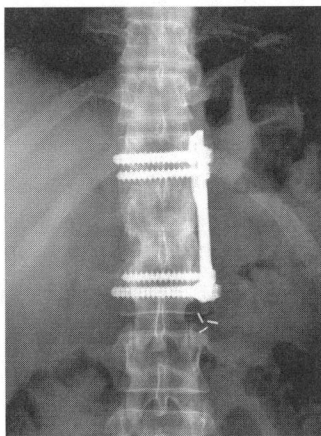

X-ray of post-op hardware.

MILE MARKER 6

Exit the Sauna
of Self-Pity

Mile Marker 6—Exit the Sauna of Self-Pity

People say I'm a pretty happy guy. Others have mentioned that I come across as a well-balanced person. Some have mentioned how positive I am and what a great attitude I have, especially for being in a wheelchair. I would like to say I'm an optimistic realist. People sometimes ask if I ever have a bad day. They want to know if I get discouraged or disheartened. The answer is, of course I do! But I try not to dwell upon it. I just keep going forward, knowing tomorrow or even the next hour will be better.

A lot of people think this go get 'em' attitude was always a part of me. They mention that it must be "natural" to be that positive. I can honestly tell you it hasn't always been that way. In fact, I used to feel sorry for myself all the time and make excuses. I would justify my thoughts and blame others for my actions. I didn't hold myself accountable and I thought it was someone else's responsibility to make things better. But my attitude about life changed forever one particular moment during my first week of rehab after they transferred me to the University of Utah.

Mom was putting my clothes in the closet next to my bed and getting things situated my first night of a three-month stay at the University of Utah rehab unit in Salt Lake City. My assigned therapist, who we'll call Jill, came in the room to meet and visit with us. We talked about what we would be doing the next few days and how we would be doing it. She was trying to help me see the big picture. She wanted to give me a different vision that led to recovery but I was one step ahead of her. I wasn't just going to recover from surgery and learn how to live life in a wheelchair; I could see myself walking out of this hospital as if nothing had happened. I kept convincing myself my condition was only temporary and it wasn't that bad. I only had to look over to my right and see my quadriplegic roommate to be convinced of this. I kept telling myself I was going to walk again, even if the experts told me otherwise. I arrogantly heard her out and listened to her plan. I thought I was being patient and polite, but looking back, it was obvious I was neither patient nor polite. I was downright impatient and rude.

When she was finished telling me everything we were going to do, I looked her straight in the eyes and proudly said, "Let's start right now!" I didn't know what I was getting myself into. Being taken aback a little she said, "This is the first time I've had a patient so eager to hurt themself."

I was ready. I wanted to start right then and there. The faster we got going the faster I could accomplish my goal. My new goal was to walk out of the hospital before the three months were up. Three months was reasonable, at least that's what I thought.

We couldn't start immediately because my body brace hadn't been made. Without the brace, I could reinjure my reconstructed back. Jill made the necessary phone call to get the brace ordered. The very next day I was fitted and measured. I felt like a piñata as they put the plaster all over my torso to get a precise measurement of my body. I wondered if they would stuff treats and goodies down me next. The plaster felt warm and slimy. It was disturbingly enjoyable. They hand-delivered my body brace the very next day. It had a hard white outer shell with soft white foam coating the inside. They first explained how it went on and how I would get into it, and then we actually did it. We did it together step-by-step as it was previously explained. With help from Jill and the brace-makers I eventually got it on.

Putting on my body brace required a lot more patience than

ability. The whole process took me just under 30 minutes.[4] It was worth the time and effort since I thought I would be able to get up and move around. Unfortunately, that wasn't their plan from the beginning. As soon as we got it fastened and secured they told me to take it off. "I just got it on," I said with surprise. "It took us thirty minutes to do it the first time. I want to get up and move around!"

"We know," Jill spoke for all of them. "Now we want you to do it yourself."

Reluctantly I undid the straps again and removed the brace from my body. I felt like I was wasting my time doing this all over again. Jill and the others stood there watching as I began the process all over again. This time I was on my own and couldn't receive any help. As expected, it took me 10 minutes longer by myself than it did with the help from others. I relearned that day that with the appropriate help from others you can always get more done than on your own.

My body brace skills were getting amazing while my dressing skills lacked proficiency. For the first two weeks, I stayed in the infamous breezy hospital-issued gowns. The gowns were convenient for the nurses but not that attractive for the patients. It was a quick strip and place-back-on procedure for them. They weren't stylish but they were an easy substitution for dressing oneself. Now that I was required to get

---

[4] I first had to undo the Velcro straps that fastened the brace together. The brace was split into two sections, a top section and a bottom section. The straps were permanently fastened to the edge of the bottom section of the brace. To fasten the brace together I had to thread the straps through the metal loops that were secured tight to the edge of the top section. I would then unfasten the straps and remove the top part from the bottom part, leaving me two separate halves to work with. Then I would roll over on one side of my body and balance myself long enough to position the bottom half of my brace underneath my back. Once in place, I could slowly roll back over onto it. I would then take the upper half of my brace and place it on top of my chest. I felt like I was getting ready for battle and putting my armor on. Now that both halves were lined up I took the straps from the bottom section and strung them back through the loops that were secured to the opposite section and fasten them to their designated spots on top. What a process!

properly dressed for the day I knew it was going to be another challenge. I thought I liked challenges so I took it head on. The first attempt to dress myself was amusing. It was actually really funny.

Normally, to put on socks, underwear, or pants I would bend over, lift my leg up, and put the item of clothing on, one foot or leg at a time. This was a simple task I had done hundreds of times before my accident. Now I was placed with the dilemma of not being able to bend or lift my leg. I couldn't bend over because of my back surgery and I couldn't lift my legs up because of my paralysis. The task of getting dressed would have to be done in bed, lying flat on my back. The key to getting dressed, I found out by process of elimination, was to start with what was easiest. That would be my shirt. I would simply put it on as I always did before my accident, but I'd just have to do it while lying down on my back. I put my shirt over my head and slid both arms through the sleeves. I then slid the shirt from my chest down to my waist. The difficult part was to shimmy the shirt down past my shoulders. I struggled most days but putting on my shirt was the easy part. The hard part came next.

After my accident, I realized my legs could bend and contort in many unusual directions I couldn't do before. I experimented with several different methods of getting dressed. One of my first experiments was grabbing my foot back toward the back of my head, like a ballerina grabbing her foot and bringing it to her head. Instead of standing I did it lying down. This one didn't work very well because after I got my foot near my head I would let go of it to put my sock or pant leg on and my leg would spring back to its original position. It wasn't working well and the therapists were standing in the corner giggling about the crazy sight. They were in no hurry to help.

They knew I would figure it out.

The next experiment worked best. I began by grabbing my foot and bringing my leg toward my chest. Folding my legs in this direction was much more natural than the other way. I would bring my leg as close to my chest as possible without it springing back down. I would wrap one arm around my leg while still holding on to the item of clothing. This way, I could hold my leg while still being able to slide my clothes onto it. I was much more efficient and fast with this method. Even though I reduced the time it took to put on my socks, underwear, and pants it still took more than 20 minutes to get them on and they were much more difficult than the shirt. I was starting to see a pattern with how long it was taking to do the most basic daily tasks. I was becoming discouraged with how much time and energy I was using just to get dressed and ready for the day, and my morning routine still wasn't over.

With paralysis, complications arise in the legs. Blood clots are one of the most common complications. In order to prevent them you have to take blood-thinner medication and also wear tights. The white hospital-issued tights looked like my mother's stockings. Not only did these stockings add a new challenge to getting dressed, they added a pinch of humility.

The first time I was ordered to put them on the only thing I could think about was that my friends could never know about this. I would never hear the end of it! This new apparel that was supposed to prevent problems kept adding new ones by making it even more difficult to get dressed. In addition to the tights I had to put on my underwear, socks, pants/sweats, shirt, and shoes. I had to repeat the process of lifting my legs and pulling them forward a total of four times. As you can imagine, it took me about an hour each day to get dressed and another 30 minutes to put on my brace those first few weeks. All that time spent getting dressed wasn't a big deal at first because I believed it was the means to an end. I thought I would be able to get out of bed, go places, and do things like I used to.

It had been about two weeks since I had been upright and out of bed. I was stir crazy and needed to get out. The doctors warned me I might pass out and/or at least experience some dizziness. I didn't care. At least I would be able to go somewhere after getting out of bed. For an active 22-year-old, two weeks in bed was enough to make anyone go crazy. I was bursting at the seams with anticipation and excitement to get out and go. I pushed the button that lifted the bed up. My body brace was on and secure. I was ready to move.

Sure enough, as if they had seen this several times before, the doctors were right. The room started to spin and I almost lost consciousness. I wasn't about to let that happen, so I took some deep breaths until the room slowed down to a standstill. I began to slowly inch my way to the side of the bed. I was barely able to lift my body high enough off the bed to slide closer to the edge. My wheelchair was waiting for me. One of the nurses was holding it so it wouldn't roll away. I hadn't used my muscles for two weeks and it was very apparent as I tried to lift my body over to the edge. They just weren't working the same as before. It's amazing how long it takes to build up your muscles and how fast they can become weak and atrophied. I was sad that my legs already looked like my little sister's arms.

Arriving at the edge of the bed caused beads of sweat to form on my forehead and my muscles quivered from exhaustion. I grabbed each leg one at a time, and lowered them softly to the side of the bed. With my legs dangling down the side of the bed I repositioned my body and leaned out toward the front of the chair. I made contact with the front end of the wheelchair, where the seat section curves down toward the foot rests, and grabbed it. When my fingers touched the cold metal of the wheelchair, it lurched away from me as if it didn't want to be disturbed. I almost lost my balance and found myself on the floor but fortunately the nurse was there and she kept it from going anywhere.

My arms were shaking and my body was being uncooperative as I lifted and pulled myself over to the awaiting chair. With a little help and encouragement from Jill and the nurses, I made a leap of faith and lifted my body across the divide from the bed to the chair. Instead of slowly lowering my body into the chair, my arms gave out just as I crossed the gap. I fell directly into my chair with a loud thump. My body relaxed as I sat slightly slumped over in my new mode of transportation. Gasping for air with perspiration trickling down my face, I turned around and reveled in the victory of overcoming my third major milestone. I discovered getting dressed and putting on my body brace was a lot easier compared to transferring from my bed to the wheelchair.

My heartrate was returning back to normal and my breathing slowed down as the reality of my accomplishment truly set in. I didn't know transferring from my bed to the chair would take so much out of me. As I looked up at the clock I became a little discouraged with what just took place. I had just transferred from my bed into my chair for the first time. I did this all by myself and succeeded in accomplishing the task. It was a bitter-sweet victory since it took me more than 10 minutes to do it.

Simple tasks were taking me a lot longer than I was accustomed to. It also dawned on me at that moment that getting out of bed was going to be easier than getting back into bed. The bed was higher than the chair and I wasn't going to be able to fall into my bed as I had just finished doing into my wheelchair. "No worries," I thought as the childhood memory adage flashed through my mind again: "For every worry under the sun, there is a solution or there is none. If there be one hurry and find it, if there be none never mind it."

My goal of walking out of the hospital, three months from now, was off to a slow start. The time it took to get dressed, to get my body brace on, and to get out of bed was starting to really discourage me to the point of breaking. Adversity was hitting me square in the face. I thought I was prepared for what was ahead, but reality came so hard and so fast. I learned there is a definite gap between what is ideal and what is real. I began to really feel sorry for myself that day and my zeal and will was truly being tested. I didn't know it at that time, but I was preparing for a party, my pity party.

After the morning therapy session ended I went back to my room and rested. I struggled back into bed, took off my body brace, and began contemplating the events that had just taken place. I was overwhelmed with the same tasks that lay ahead every day. Everything that used to be simple now became a giant chore. I couldn't even dress myself, put on my brace, and get out of bed without having to plan for it first.

Before I completely entered into the sweltering and suffocating sauna of self-pity I heard my stomach rumble. Lunch was being served in the rehab cafeteria. Food was no longer being served in bed. If I wanted to eat I had to get out of bed. I managed to get my brace on again and into my chair without any help. I rolled down the long, disinfected hall toward the lunchroom. By the time I entered through the doors I was physically exhausted. The littlest things tired me out. I was done, both physically and mentally. The tears turned on and started streaming down my cheeks. I had just entered the planet of pity and I didn't care anymore. I wanted my own pity party that day and nobody else was invited.

For the first time during rehab and my road to recovery I felt sorry for myself and thought, "Why me?" I picked up my tray and got my food, oblivious to the world around me. With my tray loaded with food I sat down at the table situated as far away as possible from anybody else. I wanted to hole up and be by myself and wallow in my sweet, sugary, sticky mess of self-pity. For some reason, I had positioned myself straight across from the only other patient at the table. Tears continued to roll down my cheeks and drop onto my shirt and lap as I positioned my chair underneath the table. I picked up my fork and was about to eat away my sorrows when I heard a faint voice. This muffled voice brought me back to reality. It snapped me out of my pity party and was coming from the patient directly across the table.

In his slurred and struggling speech he asked, "Wath... wong...duth? Why' a...cyaing?" Interpreted as, "What's wrong dude, why ya crying?" Instantly my tears turned off, stopping the streams that were previously running down my cheeks. My sobs went away and I left the destructive and debilitating world of self-pity. This voice belonged to a man who had it worse than me. A man who innocently wanted to know what was so bad in my life to cause me such emotion.

That moment changed my life and my future forever. That moment of clarity affected me the deepest during this trial. That simple but direct question took me from my pity party and brought me back to reality. It was the catalyst that caused me to look around and see what was really going on. Something clicked inside my head and I stopped thinking about myself for the first time since arriving at the hospital. I thought I was the only one with problems. I thought I was the only one who had it tough. I instantly realized my world wasn't that tough. It was easy compared to the guy at the other end of the table who had to have somebody else feed him because his arms wouldn't move. My world was easy compared to the woman on the opposite end of the room who had a feeding tube stuck down her throat because she couldn't chew and swallow. My world was easy compared to the man whose fork was wrapped around his hand because his fingers no longer worked. My reality wasn't hard compared to the guy sitting directly across from me who could barely feed himself and slurred as he talked.

I realized things could be worse than taking an hour and a half to get dressed and not being able to move like I once did. I knew there were thousands if not millions who had it worse than me and I needed to be grateful for what I did have. Instead of feeling sorry for myself I began to experience genuine empathy for others. I sincerely wanted to know how I might help others in their own time of need. It was clear what I needed to do.

"Nothing's wrong," I replied to the stranger sitting across from me. "Actually, everything's quite all right," I continued with added courage and strength.

The warm feeling of reassurance that follows after making the right decision entered my body and warmed me right up. My heart was full and my burdens were lightened. I knew from that point on everything would be alright. I just knew it. I haven't had another pity party like it since. I had journeyed through the recesses of darkness, doubt, and despair and had entered into the spacious realm of light, hope, and trust rarely to return to discouragement again. I had decided then and there all would be well.

I invite you to memorize the following couplet and look outside yourself and SWAT someone. SWAT means Serve

82

Without A Trace. Look outside yourself and beyond your limits for simple ways to help others around you. Open a door for someone. Tell someone they look nice today. Be the first to ask "What's wrong? How can I help?" Be the one to smile at a stranger. After all, *"A smile is a crooked line that sets things straight!"* ☺ That's a wise insight from my brother, Chris Griffin.

S.W.A.T. with a Smile

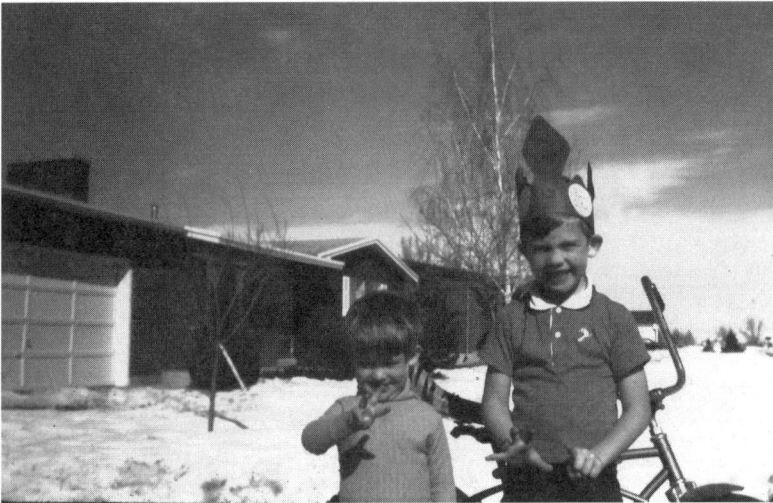

King for just one day with my younger brother Chris, ages 3 and 6.

MILE MARKER 7

Hope for a
Better Day

Mile Marker 7–Hope for a Better Day

My weeklong stay at McKay Dee hospital was short-lived. The personnel were very professional and they did an excellent job taking care of me. I couldn't stay there forever because I needed to begin the hard road to recovery with therapy. I was transferred to the University of Utah's Rehab facility located 36 miles south of Ogden in Salt Lake City. The support I had received from family, friends, doctors, nurses, and even complete strangers (who later became friends) was priceless. They were a major part of the patch-up process for healing. I called them my support team.

After the visitors who had consistently streamed into my room and put a smile on my face for the first seven days had slowed to a trickle. I hesitantly took down the postcards that decorated my room. Flowers that once brightened my burdens and brought happiness and hope to my life were given to family members and taken home. The phone calls, flowers, letters, and cards from my support team had kept me optimistic and focused. They kept me focused on the good and positive things in life. These kind acts of selfless service kept the darkness and depression away. They expanded the light, increased the hope, improved the optimism, and brought peace into my life. My support system I had in Ogden was incredible but they were gone now and I felt alone.

Have you ever been alone? I mean really alone? Where you feel like nobody knows you exist. Or even worse, they don't even care that you exist? Have you ever wondered if anyone would ever recognize you for you? Have you pondered the idea that you may never have a friend or, worse yet, an intimate relationship? There are 7 billion people in this world. You would think we would be able to find someone out there, right?

So why do we feel so lonely and inadequate at times?

When I arrived at the University of Utah's rehab facility I wasn't prepared for the dramatic change that would come into my world. The drop off in the number of my visitors was the first adjustment. At first, I was mad at how few there were, but I couldn't really be angry at them because everyone who came to visit me lived 80 miles away in Cache Valley. People were busy with work, school, and other activities and I knew it was 40 miles farther than before. I understood it was harder for people to come visit me, but it still hurt to be alone.

I was awakened again by one of the "vampires" as I liked to call them One of the technicians was there to draw more blood. "Why do they come at the weirdest and most inconvenient hours," I complained to myself as they drew my blood. It's pretty hard to get any rest when the vampires wake you up in the middle of the night. Getting what she came for, the technician gathered her equipment and silently left the room. I was left all alone with my thoughts. That's usually not a good thing in the middle of the night. There have been some pretty lonely moments in my life but nothing compared to this time. During previous lonely moments I had wandered the dark empty halls of doubt and despair. It was pitch black outside and I momentarily wondered what time it really was.

I was awake now so I decided to take that mental walk down the cranium corridor of depression. I arrived at Room R: Relationships, and hesitated before going in. "What the heck," I thought to myself. "I'll only go in for a second." I forcefully pushed open the doors, walked through them, and instantly changed my mind. I normally avoided this room because of the hurt it caused but tonight it was more inviting than others. I was so tired and discouraged I didn't care what I was about to see. I knew I was going to stay a while when I mentally sat down next to the desk in the middle of the room and assessed what was around the dark and cluttered room. I wanted answers and I wanted clarity. I wanted to know if it would ever be possible to be with someone, to have a relationship, to have a wife, or to even have children. Tonight, it seemed impossible!

My accident left me paralyzed. I had no movement whatsoever. I couldn't feel anything or move anything from the waist down. For a 22-year-old man, no sensation or movement below the belt was a life sentence, especially for one who committed to exercise virtue and chastity until marriage. I believed in God and I believed He wanted me to live a happy life. I was taught that principle by my parents and I thought I knew it for myself. I was taught part of our happiness comes from living a clean and virtuous life. Abstaining and being clean hasn't always been easy, especially when others around you think the opposite. Happiness to others seems to mean doing whatever you want as long as it's consensual or it doesn't affect anyone else. It seems impossible to keep higher standards when everyone around you has lowered theirs. "I thought good things were supposed to happen to good people," I began to question.

I looked around the dark and empty room in my mind and spotted a place where some of my past relationships had been. There were some surprisingly sweet memories on my memory wall. The first relationship memory I came to was the portrait of my neighborhood sweetheart. The pre-kindergarten crush made me smile. Our older brothers and sisters would always try and get us to kiss. There were other innocent relationship portraits on the wall as well. The ones where you do stupid things like pull their hair, say something outrageous, or even do something irrational just to get their attention. There were the memories of when my friends and I would go to the roller skating rink and wait for the moments when it was the girls turn to ask the boys to skate. Holding hands was an exciting time for a young boy.

Not all the portraits contained sweet and kind memories, though. There was one memory in particular that happened in fourth or fifth grade that still stings when I think of it. It was the day when everyone received their school pictures and exchanged them with each other, especially with those we liked. This year I was going to exchange pictures with the girls I thought were cute because in years past I could never muster enough courage to do it. I didn't need to do it because three of the cutest and most popular girls in the class came up to me and asked me for a picture. I was on cloud nine. I cut out my pictures with precision. I wanted them to be perfect for these girls. I cut them out and delivered all three with pride in my heart. "Someone likes me," I thought as I walked away.

A few hours later I looked up from my homework and those three girls were standing next to my desk. I thought for a moment they were bringing a picture of their own to give to me. They did give me a picture, but it wasn't theirs. It was mine. They had ripped it up into what appeared a million pieces. They dropped the shreds onto my desk and walked away giggling. I watched in slow motion as the pieces slowly fluttered down to my desk. It felt like my heart had been ripped up and thrown away instead of my pictures. I was crushed and hurt beyond words.

I was very hesitant with girls after that. It was painstakingly difficult to put myself out there and trust any girl. Girls made me really nervous after that but I made sure I wouldn't let that experience snuff out the flames of fervor either. I stumbled through high school but still dated and had a small number of good experiences. I continued to stay chaste while being chased through college.

I'm not saying I was perfect or innocent the whole time. I did some foolish things most teenage boys do but for the most part I maintained God's standards uprightly and honorably. So why was I now placed in this situation where the very thing I was trying to save was taken away? Why did I commit to invest in something when I wasn't guaranteed to withdraw from it in the future? I felt cheated.

My anger rose and I wanted to throw files of paper in the air and swipe off the perfectly organized desk in the imaginary room. I wanted to upturn the chairs and shatter the delicate pieces of art in Room R. I was so upset and angry at that moment. I wasn't quite sure where it originated from but I did know I was foaming at the mouth and ready to hurt someone.

I believe these emotions were triggered by a conversation I had had with my nurse 12 hours earlier. She came in to talk with me that afternoon. She thoughtfully wondered if I had any questions I wanted answered. The only question I really had was, "Will I ever be able to have a sexual relationship?" The doctors explained earlier that with a spinal cord injury the sexual function of the body was the first to go and the last to come back. She didn't have an answer but suggested I watch an educational video on disabled body relationships. I graciously declined, not wanting to sear my mind with those memories. However, my question and concern was sincere and far from perversion. I honestly wanted to know if I would be able to do that which is most sacred and symbolic to the soul. I wanted to know if I would ever be able to do the impossible and have children.

In my youth I was taught that being chaste is what God wanted me to be. As a teenager and young adult, I chose to be chaste for myself. Now that I was paralyzed and felt I hadn't been given a choice, I was mad. At least those were my initial feelings. I was angry, upset, confused, discouraged, and even depressed. I could remain in this state of mind or I could change it. Even the darkest of nights are accompanied with the brightest of dawns. I believe even the bleakest moments can be turned into the brightest and sweetest memories of our lives, if we choose to see it that way. Our world is what we make of it. We create what we want to see or what we've been told to see. I believe our minds are stronger than medication. In fact, our mind and body can produce the chemicals found in most medications. Daniel Coyle in his book called *The Talent Code*. refers to this power within our minds and the influence it has with our surroundings the following way:

Dr. Albert Ellis's approach, combined with that of Dr. Aaron Beck, became known as cognitive-behavioral therapy, which has been shown, according to *The New York Times*, to be equal to or better than prescription drugs for combating depression, anxiety, and obsessive-compulsive disorder.

His ideas weren't new. They came from philosophers like Epictetus, who said, "It's not events, but our opinions about them, which cause us suffering."[5]

Science has shown that it's not just nature or nurture which creates the world we presently live in but our minds. The programing we received from our parents and the thoughts we developed from our past have a far greater effect on our current situation than we think. Our past experiences make it very difficult to change the future because our current experiences validate our present mindset; which was developed by our past. This truth is another one of life's many paradoxes. Yet, if this is true, then the real question that needs to be

---

[5]Ellis, who died in 2007, was named the second most influential psychologist of the Twentieth Century by the American Psychological Association. (Carl Rogers was first and Sigmund Freud was third.)

answered is, if we don't like what we're getting out of our lives, then what are we putting or allowing to be put into our minds? The world we choose to live in is created by our minds.

My mental room of gloom and doom was created and copied from the images I had seen or was told about from the past. Most of those thoughts and images had come from the movies and TV shows I'd watched. Others had come from the countless songs I'd listened to over the years. Unfortunately, most of those images, songs, and shows contained negative messages that were contrary to the ideals of a truly happy life. Fortunately, there were a few good images, songs, and shows I had heard and seen as well. These things, accompanied by reading good books and being taught by great people, had helped instill enough positive energy, images, and thoughts to get me through this night. The good books I read most, came from the "good book" of God. Not the books about God, but the books from God.

I left Room R and returned to reality. The sun was coming through the windows and it was going to be a better day today. I was going to make it a better day by how I thought and what I said. I may never have the relationship I dreamed about but I was going to dream about having better relationships. I would let go of the impossible and focus on the possible. I wasn't going to continue looking back and dwelling on the things I couldn't change. Instead, I was going to focus forward and start working on the things I could change. I was going to focus on what I could control. I was going to make the choice to continue to cultivate the relationships I did have and prepare myself for the ones I might have. I would continue to hope for a better day by hopefully being better today. I'm possible!

If you're not happy with your present conditions, I invite you to do a few things differently. We are only a thought away

91

from changing our lives. I invite you to be a little more positive than in the past. I invite you to make a simple change by simply changing the way you think. Eliminate the words "I Can't," and replace them with "I Can!" Take that step today and repeat the positive phrases of affirmation right before you go to bed and immediately after you wake up. Commit to make it a part of your praying and pondering routine. You're possible!

Watch the Sun Rise and Think

Affirmation Phrases
www.griffinmotivation.com/affirmation

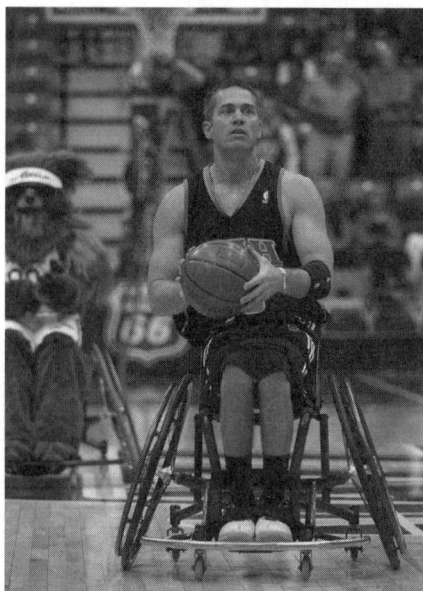

Wheelin' Jazz exhibition during halftime of a Utah Jazz game.

Being awarded a certificate for the Guinness
Book of World Records.

I CAN...!

93

MILE MARKER 8

Attitude Is Positively
Everything

Mile Marker 8—Attitude Is Positively Everything

Although my attitude had significantly been adjusted, I still had to deal with the down days that came with life. Life in the rehab center was a reflection of the sterile white walls that surrounded me on a daily basis. There wasn't much color or variation in the day-to-day activities and exercises. It required a lot of effort to focus on the good things that took place in the hospital. The days were going by slowly. Minutes seemed like hours. Hours seemed like days. Days seemed like weeks. And weeks seemed like months. It was the same routine day in and day out. In order to help me through these vanilla dull days, I needed to be precise with the fundamentals of a happy hospital life. I needed to get up early and on time. I needed to exercise every day. I needed to be polite and kind even when I hurt and wasn't feeling well. I needed to stay focus on my goals. I knew I didn't just want to do them by going through the motions but I wanted to do them right and with the right intention.

I desired to do great things, but more importantly I desired to be great. I started to understand that great human beings accomplish great things. This doesn't mean great things have only been accomplished by great people, but great people always accomplish great things. I didn't know exactly what I wanted to do at this point in the hospital, but I knew I wanted to do whatever it was right, without cutting corners. I learned shortcuts are different paths we take when we expect to give less and hope to receive more. If shortcuts are taken, no matter what the outcome is, the crack will always occur. If we can't do it right the first time, when will we find the time to do it over?

I've learned for myself that cutting corners leads nowhere but down.

I wanted to take advantage of the time I had in rehab and remain focused on the prize. The prize was getting better and moving forward with a positive attitude. I wanted to create a "battle-cry," a mission statement that summed up what I really wanted. I wanted something that would motivate me to maintain my focus on the fundamentals. I wanted something to help me during the daily drudgery. There are times when the grind of things we do daily becomes overwhelming and unbearable and we don't want to continue. I wanted this battle-cry to be reflected in my own life's work. If I could clearly define it and do it right, then perhaps I could help others learn from it as well.

I wanted to establish and define a concept others could duplicate. I wanted to help others who would come after me to learn from my mistakes and follow a route that will get them further than they currently are, while also doing it faster. One example is the Wright brothers. The Wright brothers didn't invent aviation, they just packaged it properly. Orville and Wilbur's fixed-wing aircraft–a kite mounted on a stick–was conceived and flown almost a century before they made their famous first flight. The Wright brothers didn't come up with the flying concept, but they did come up with the concept that took flight. People were flying all sorts of things at that time but the Wright brothers were the first to design and build a flying craft that could be controlled while in the air. Every successful aircraft built since, beginning with the 1902 Wright glider, has had controls to roll the wings right or left, pitch the nose up or down, and yaw the nose from side to side. The Wright boys harnessed the airways and took control of their dream (flight).

"Before the Wright Brothers, no one in aviation did anything fundamentally right. Since the Wright Brothers, no one has done anything fundamentally different."[6] The Wrights created and packaged a way to fly that has allowed mankind to go places thought to be impossible. They not only created something that helped other pilots' dreams take flight, but also gave vision to everyone else who has taken that flight. They've helped us see the world in ways it had never been seen before.

Today's planes are much more complex and need specialized instruments to help maneuver and control them. The instrument that gets the plane from one place to another is called the "attitude meter." Similar to what's happened to the plane has happened to our lives. Life has become complicated and we need something to guide us and direct us. In order to get where we want to go we must address and adjust our own attitude meter.

"Stay positive," I thought as I reflected on what my battle-cry would be. It didn't come instantly but I knew it would eventually come if I kept at it and stayed positive. To stay positive my attitude consistently needed to be addressed and adjusted. I needed to be reminded of what I really wanted. Attitude is the ground control to everything else we do. Attitude affects our thoughts, our thoughts affect our words, our words affect our behavior, and our behavior determines our character. Character is the summation of what we have done and who we have become. Our character is a reflection of our attitude. Attitude works best when we vigilantly look for and trust the small and subtle nudges that come from a higher power. Attitude works best when we keep an open heart to receive those sacred suggestions. Positive attitude is cultivated

---

[6]Darrel Collins, US Park Service, Kitty Hawk National Historical Park.

by giving simple, silent, and self-effacing service. Positive attitude increases and expands when we allow our minds time to meditate, ponder, and pray. Attitude works best when we have the courage to make those small changes we see, hear, and feel. Attitude is what guides us to become great. Great people create and accomplish great things. Greatness doesn't happen overnight. Greatness comes with practice. Greatness requires effort. Everything worthwhile in life requires effort. Commit yourself to being great!

DOn't qu**IT** and stay positive became my personal battle-cry. It became clear to me that it was essential to have this don't quit attitude as I went through the sterile, mundane, and colorless routines and activities of hospital life. Though not exciting, the next few months did give me invaluable time to practice for future difficult skirmishes.

Each day when I woke up, or more like when I got woken up early by one of the nurses, I would be given my daily shot of blood thinner. The nurses injected the medication through my stomach. They were very precise and consistent with when and where they gave me the shot. They would pick a different spot on my stomach to inject the medicine to keep me from bruising. I dreaded this time of the morning because I enjoyed my sleep and disliked the pain. It felt like I was being stung by a bee. I tried to practice positive thinking each morning by telling myself the pain was only temporary and the nurses knew what they were doing. I still thought there had to be a better way. It took two weeks of early morning torture to discover a better way. I was so happy I listened and figured it out.

There was this definite, distinct, and well-defined line on my stomach that separated the area where I could feel and where I could not feel. The line was located about 2 inches below my belly button. The nurses would give me the shots above this line every time. The idea of having them give me the shot lower came to me one quiet morning while contemplating their arrival. It was simple and clear to me with the thought, "If the nurses would inject the medicine one inch lower you wouldn't be able to feel it because of the paralysis."

When the nurse walked in to give me the shot I asked, "Is there any reason why you couldn't give me that shot any lower?"

"No, not at all," she quietly whispered, keeping her voice down to avoid waking up the other patients in the room. "Where would you like it," she asked.

"Anywhere I can't feel would be nice." From that day forward, I didn't receive another shot I didn't like. The mornings were more enjoyable and the bee stings went away. The results of looking for the positive and searching for a solution were paying off. I even started seeing some of the benefits of being paralyzed.

The daily routine started with the shots but it didn't stop there. After I got dressed and finished the restroom ritual I would roll down to the lunchroom and eat breakfast. As I rolled on by I would greet the nurses and other patients with a friendly "hello." After the feeding frenzy was over and I was full, I would roll back to my room, get back in bed, and watch SportsCenter while I waited for my therapist, who we'll call Joe, to begin the morning stretches. When Joe would come and do my leg stretches in the morning, we tended to watch more than we worked. We didn't get much done because SportsCenter highlights were more intriguing than stretching. We got distracted and lost focus.

On the other hand, when Tina, the other therapist, did the morning stretches, SportsCenter was forgotten. I didn't get to watch as nearly as many highlights as I did when Joe was there. Tina thought it was better that I make some highlights of my own. Some days I thought there should have been a camera there to catch all the moves and misery of the day. I was definitely worked over and more exhausted with Tina than Joe. I learned practice doesn't make perfect unless I perfectly practice. Tina helped me focus when I didn't want to work and motivated me to continue when I wanted to quit. A master mentor will always get you to accomplish more than is prescribed.

The routine only began to heat up at this point. The stretches were only the beginning. After the therapist left, I would put my body brace back on, transfer into my chair, and head downstairs to the therapy room for my morning session. I discovered very quickly -there is more than physical therapy. I wasn't aware there was vocational therapy, recreational therapy, occupational therapy, and many other kinds of therapy. The morning session was set apart as the physical component of my therapy. This was consistently a time to be humbled and to be brought back to reality. While lying on my bed in my room I would constantly dream about all the improvements that needed to happen in order for me to walk out of the hospital. After some time of visualizing myself walking, I would catch myself believing I had actually improved to the point I was just one day away from fulfilling my dream. Those morning therapy sessions absolutely humbled me.

"Griff, let's go. You've got two more sets!" my therapist insisted. Her voice brought me back from my wayward thoughts and back into the proverbial frying pan. There were many times I didn't know why I was there. I couldn't do three-fourths of the exercises they had me doing. For me, morning therapy sessions were more about flirting with the ladies than keeping my legs from atrophying more than they already had.

By this time my legs were pretty much looking like the twigs from a November tree whose leaves had fallen off. They definitely weren't the legs of a football receiver. To add insult to injury, I found out my flirting skills were more of a lost cause than my legs were.

When I completed the morning therapy session I would take a quick break and rest on my bed again. I believe I watched more TV during those two months in the hospital than I had my whole life put together. It was pathetic. I knew what program was scheduled, what channel it was on, and when it was showing. I was the rolling portable TV guide. I would willingly get out of bed for the important things like breakfast, lunch, and dinner. But for all the other things that made me hurt or doubt, I would dread the moment when I would have to turn off the TV and drag myself out of bed. Turning off the TV is the best thing anyone can do to begin seeing the positive around them. Unfortunately, I wasn't quite ready to give up this comfort.

Even though my leg muscles were melting away and didn't function, I still had half my body that worked. I would end the day with another session of physical therapy. This included some exercises like lifting weights or pedaling the hand machine. I liked lifting weights because when I was finished I could sit and admire the size of my arms. Using my arms to push myself around, transfer to and from my chair, and everything else bulked and chiseled my upper body. Those muscles were getting bigger and stronger every day.

After getting cleaned up I would end the daily routine with dinner and a lazy stroll around the hospital before returning to my bed to watch more TV. Occasionally I would get a visitor or two but that was the exception and not the rule.

This routine happened every single day. It was like

101

clockwork–predictable and exact. It was starting to get boring. In order to break up the monotony of the routine I would venture off, when I wasn't scheduled for therapy, to some remote part of the hospital. I would eventually gravitate to areas of the hospital that would uplift and strengthen my resolve. I would often go to the pediatric ward and visit some of the children. Other times I would find myself in the women's ward and I would sit and admire the recent newcomers to our world. The innocent and peaceful newborn babies looked so cuddly and warm. I wanted to reach out and hold them as I peered through the glass wall.

These daily adventures helped me refocus. Occasionally I would go out to the front entrance of the hospital where the air was refreshing, the sounds of the water fountain invigorating, and the people coming and going were interesting to observe. I would take my Calvin and Hobbs comic book and sit there for hours reading and enjoying the warm weather. This was a great place to do some additional leg exercises and it also provided cheap entertainment. The front entrance was a happening place. I really enjoyed my time out front. I could sit and watch people while they came and went. After a while I was able to get a pretty good read on which ones were coming to the hospital because they had just received bad news about a loved one or if they were just coming to lift another's spirits and help them recover from their ailments. I learned our body language says a lot about how we're feeling. It speaks volumes of what we are thinking. Think positive!

During the days I didn't feel like reading or doing my leg exercises I would attempt to diagnose what kind of ailment or condition the visitors and patients had as they walked past me and into the hospital.

"Social," was the diagnosis of one person's problem as

they walked past. The greasy slicked back hair and the pocket protector completely full of pens and pieces of paper gave that one away. At least that is what I perceived it to be.

"Mental, definitely mental," I thought as the next person walked past talking to themselves. I couldn't quite make out the mumbling and I tried to interpret whether they were cursing, trying to give themselves a pep-talk, or just giving themselves an old-fashioned tongue lashing. Whatever it was, I was having fun diagnosing the problem and I was great at it.

"Physical," was the next diagnosis. I couldn't be mistaken on this one, not with his arm twisted like that.

This would go on for hours. It wasn't until a few of my "patients" did a double-take of their own that I realized I probably shouldn't be judging these people's problems and giving them a label that doesn't belong. I had a lot of audacity to judge others while I sat in my wheelchair wearing blue sweat pants, a white turtle-shell body brace for a shirt, a blue ball cap worn backward, holding a comic book in hand accompanied by crazy facial expressions while doing leg exercises. Now I was a sight to see!

My self-proclaimed patients would walk past and glance over at me as they headed toward the hospital entrance. Before entering, they would double-take and look back to get a better look at the "thing" that was sitting in the wheelchair with a comic book on its lap and sweat running down its distorted face. They were probably thinking, "Somebody needs to get that guy back to the mental ward." I could read it from their expressions. They were right! I did need to get back to the mental ward. I needed to do something different, something positive. I needed to be constructive, not destructive.

I needed to get back to the mental ward to readjust my attitude. I thought by pointing out other people's problems I was momentarily able to forget about my own. This seemed okay at first, but having a good time or an innocent little laugh at another person's expense is wrong. It was as if I wanted to be better than them, so to be better than them I had to make them less than me. If I made fun of them or tore them down, it would technically leave me above them. In reality, all it did was leave me feeling down and depressed. Taking some time to step back and reassess the situation, I realized I could be at the top but get there a different way. Instead of belittling or tearing other people down, I could encourage and lift others up. I cannot bring others to higher ground unless I am standing on it first. In the future I would lift instead of tear down. I would encourage instead of discourage. I would look for the positive instead of pointing out the negative. This would require effort and discipline but it would make both of us better. My attitude meter had been set and programmed to be positively better.

The drudgery of the daily routine was getting to me but I wasn't going to let it beat me. I needed to make a few changes for this to happen. I needed to get out of this environment before I accepted it as normal. I needed my support team back. I needed to keep my eyes on the prize and visualize. I needed to remind myself that the prize was my dream and my dream was to walk again. My sights were set. My bearings and attitude were readjusted. I was going to do it the right way without using shortcuts. I was going to raise my sights to higher ground. I was going to DO IT!

I invite you to adjust your attitude by a fraction. I invite you to perfectly practice being positive. Commit each morning and night to continue to meditate, ponder, and pray. Reconnect with the Source of all good things so you may regain control of the areas of your life you need to adjust. This will enable you to soar higher, travel longer distances, and arrive at the destination of your desires.

Attitude Meter
www.griffinmotivation.com/attitude

Jeff Griffin giving back to others around the world.

MILE MARKER 9

Seeing the Signs

Mile Marker 9–Seeing the Signs

With my attitude adjusted and mind cleared of doubt, I was ready to move forward. I needed to keep my eyes half-closed and my mind wide open. I could use all the available space in my mind to store positive thoughts and any other possibilities that would lead to my success. I needed to look for signs of improvement and progression. These small signs are subtle and can be overlooked very easily if we're not paying attention. If you don't purposely look for them they may slip right on by without you noticing they were given to help. The little things in life often make the biggest impact, especially during the difficult times. Signs of improvement and progression will fan the flames of desire to motivate us forward. Look for them!

It had been about a month since the doctors had done their diagnostics on my legs to determine my level of paralysis. The method they used was a very high-tech procedure. It was done with a very expensive instrument and was carried out with accurate measurements. The instrument the doctors used was a medium sized safety pin. I was being facetious about how expensive the instrument was because it was such a simple item for such a serious diagnosis. They wanted to determine how much feeling had returned to my legs, if any, since the surgery. Once their findings were finished and finalized they would write up the results and put them on record as their expert opinions. This was serious stuff! What doctors have to say can be pretty impactful and have a lasting effect on what you do from there on out. I hoped they would get it right.

They began the test by doing the first of three options to determine the feeling I had in my legs. First was to stab the skin of the patient, which was me, with the sharp end of the pin to see if I could feel pain. Their second option was to stab me with the blunt end of the pin using the same downward motion as before to determine if I could feel any sensation at all. The third and final option was to do nothing at all. They would imitate the same downward motion as before, pretending to poke my legs with the pin but actually do nothing to see if you were guessing the whole time or not. I was going to try my hardest to get it right. I was going to manipulate the test if I had to. I just wanted a good diagnosis. I later learned that cheating on anything will get you in trouble and contaminate the signs that can help you the most.

I failed the test miserably. I couldn't feel a thing so I did what I used to do in high school while taking tests: I guessed. I figured I had a 1-in-3 chance of getting it right. Unfortunately, I didn't get it right. The doctors recorded their findings and made it official. They determined I couldn't feel or use any part of my legs. I felt like it was too early for such a declaration. I hate it when someone snuffs out any rays of hope and light. I especially hate it when a leader or even a doctor pronounces what is and what will be forever without giving any other options. Give us some hope! Who knows what could happen in five or ten years? There are too many unknowns out there. They never painted a pretty picture for me. It seemed paramount that they tell me the impossible without caring about the possible. The vision of the future had again been painted for me by others. I had a choice to make. Either I could listen to them and believe what they were telling me or I could paint my own picture, use my own colors, set my own goals, and accomplish them while watching for the signs of improvement. I chose the latter.

Three weeks had gone by with my daily routine of exercising being accomplished. I added some extra exercises on the side, without the nurses and therapists knowing about it. I was hoping for a speedy recovery and faster results. Unfortunately, the expected results didn't come and I saw no improvement. Doubt and fear crept in again, darkening my dream and vision just a little bit. My faith and resolve were continually being tested. I decided I needed a warm shower to wash away my frustrations. The morning shower was where I recognized one of the first signs of improvement.

I rolled into the shower room and positioned my wheelchair next to the white padded shower chair. I slowly removed my clothes, noticing again how much more effort it required to do a simple task. I finally finished getting my clothes off, transferred to the shower chair, and turned on the water. I was enjoying the warm water as it hit my head and flowed down my back. I rolled my shoulders forward, bowed my head, and put my arms on the handrail to fully relax my body. As the water rolled down my back, soft ripples of pleasure traveled contrary to the water and back up to my brain. I was enjoying my shower and allowing all my frustrations to tumble away and go down the drain when I noticed the slight sign of change.

The water that was rolling down my back was also cascading over my shoulders and hitting my legs. I could actually feel the water droplets hitting my thighs. Initially I thought my mind was playing tricks on me but I knew it couldn't be. For the past three weeks, I had taken a shower without any feeling in my thighs; they were numb from the paralysis. However, this morning was different.

Since I could feel the water hitting my legs I decided to do an experiment. I decided to turn the handle toward the cold position to see if my legs could distinguish the change in temperature as well. If they could, I knew I wasn't delusional. I turned the shower handle clockwise expecting cold water to

109

come out. Apparently, I turned the handle the wrong way or the plumber put the handle on wrong. Instead of freezing-cold water coming out, scalding hot water poured onto my legs. I let out a curdling scream that was as hot as the water hitting my legs. My brain registered what had just happened, while my body was trying to cope with the new sensation. "Ooouuch!" I thought as I quickly reached up to the shower handle and cranked it all the way the other direction. For a brief instant, relief came to my legs as the ice-cold water shot out of the nozzle and onto my legs. "Ooohh," I shouted again as my legs registered the cold temperature of the water hitting them. My upper body was screaming for relief so I quickly readjusted the handle. Warm water covered my whole body again. The parody of the situation was hitting me straight in the eyes. I was burning and freezing within a few seconds of each other. Both were very unpleasant to my legs but at the same time very exhilarating and exciting to my soul. I could feel hot and cold temperatures on the upper middle part of my thighs.

The straw-width area I could feel on my thigh ran all the way to my knees. I was about to celebrate my new discovery when one of the nurses, who had heard my screams, came running in to where I was showering. "Aauggggh" I shouted one last time as she came barging in to see what the screaming was all about. I was thrilled at the small sign of improvement that had been revealed, dispelling the doubt and fear that was starting to darken my dreams of walking again. The water droplets on my legs that day were like rays of sunlight penetrating the stormy skies, giving me slivers of hope.

Another sign that gave me hope and courage to keep fighting was the amount of time I stayed up on my feet while working the parallel bars. Every day I would get dressed and go downstairs to do physical therapy. Therapy consisted of several different exercises. All the exercises we did in physical therapy (PT) were focused on my legs. The most common exercises were proper transferring skills, leg lifts, leg extensions, and the parallel bars. All these exercises were done with the aid of the physical therapist.

So far I was not making much progress with the leg lifts and extensions. The problem was the muscles in my legs didn't work. When the therapist asked me to lift my leg, my brain would tell it to lift but my leg would not obey. This unwilful disobedience would not stop my leg from lifting, however, because the therapist would grab my sweat pants and lift my leg for me. By the time we were done with that exercise both of us would have sweat rolling down our foreheads.

The same procedure was followed when we did leg extensions. I was told to extend my leg to the side. Being the perfect patient I was, I would comply or at least try. I would tell my leg to move away from my body but it could not do it on its own. The therapist would again grab my sweats and move my leg out for me. I of course did not just lay there and let them do all the work. I would mentally exert all the energy I had to move my leg. I was exhausted by the time we were finished with those two exercises. After the leg extensions and lifts were over I would transfer into the wheelchair and move to the parallel bars.

Before I could use the parallel bars, I had to put plastic leg braces on my legs for support. While I took my shoes off and slid my feet into the brace a smile crept on my face as I thought of my friends calling me "Forest Gump." I could hear them now shouting out to me, "Run Griffin, run!" I secured the braces on my legs, put my shoes back on, and positioned myself in-between the parallel bars. The first time I pulled myself upright to a standing position took about five minutes. I had lost all the strength in my legs, and my arms and shoulders had lost some muscle strength as well. It took a while to figure out how to do it but I eventually did. Once up, the therapist would have me look at the mirror in front of me and concentrate on trying to walk from one end of the bars to the other. I would command my legs to lift and move forward but they wouldn't obey. I still moved forward because the therapist picked up my legs and moved them forward for me. It felt great to be up on my feet. I had flashbacks of before my accident when I was standing. It was nice to look people straight in the eyes instead of looking up at them.

After I went back and forth a few times on the parallel bars with the help of my therapist, I practiced letting go of the bars and counting how long I could keep my balance without having to grab them again. The idea was to see how long I could stand, but the reality was whether I would grab the bars again before crashing to the floor. The first time I tried this exercise I set a baseline time of 1.3 seconds. That was my personal best. Before we finished that day, I had improved my time to a solid 5 seconds. I was excited and ready to go forward and to improve.

Like working toward most goals, something unexpected happened that would set me back for a while. When I was doing the exercise for the last time that day I pulled my groin muscle where the upper leg meets the hip. I didn't feel it happen but it was so bad it caused me to be in bed for a week. I couldn't even get out of bed to go eat. This injury didn't make sense to me. First of all, how could I feel the injury while being paralyzed, and second, how could I actually pull a paralyzed muscle? Apparently, both were possible. It was so frustrating that I couldn't get downstairs to do my exercises. I knew my exercises would help me achieve my goal. My goal was to walk out of the hospital when I left. I was determined to do those exercises, but my body wasn't willing. I received some help from the nurses to get out of bed, but as soon as they bent my waist to a sitting position the pain would shoot through my body again. It wouldn't go away unless I lied back down in bed. I didn't want to give up so the doctors tried to freeze the area with some cold spray. It helped for a few minutes but by the time I got downstairs the muscles would warm up, the spray would wear off, and the pain would come back. My mind was willing but my body was weak and I couldn't do it, yet! It was a very long week. Again, doubt and fear slowly seeped back into my mind and made life a little bit darker. However, this time I was more prepared to deal with it. I simply looked for the signs of improvement.

Eventually I got to the point I could get out of bed and go downstairs. I was able to start my exercises again. I was able to stand back up between the parallel bars. Life was looking up again. My personal bests between the bars were improving by leaps and bounds. I was able to let go of the parallel bars and stand for 30 seconds now. The improvement was fantastic. When my mom came down on a Wednesday, I told her the great news. My appointment with the surgeon who repaired my back was coming up as well and couldn't wait to tell him too. In fact, by the time I was supposed to see him I had improved all the way to 45 seconds, without hands.

I rolled into the surgeon's office and waited impatiently to tell him the great news. I couldn't read the magazines that were placed neatly around the center table. The fish were swimming around inside the tank and darting in and out of the rocks seemed as excited as I was to talk to the doctor. I wanted to tell him about all the improvements that took place over the last couple weeks. I expected him to congratulate me on all the hard work I had done. I expected him to encourage me to continue what I was doing so my body would heal properly and my legs would regain sensation and mobility.

My name was finally called and I rolled into his office, with my mom following right behind. The doctor started with the traditional small talk then finally asked how I was doing. I immediately told him about the signs of my success and the improvement I was experiencing with the parallel bars. Waiting patiently for me to finish, the surgeon looked me straight in the eyes and said, "Don't get your hopes up. You'll never move your legs or walk again in your life."

I couldn't believe my ears. I was stunned to silence. The surgeon took all my faith and hope and shoved it down the toilet. I had already lost so much. Did he want to take away the only thing I had left? Hope? I had just been given two options. One, I could listen to the advice from this expert who spent years studying and training to fix people and who had been inside my body and seen the damage that was done. Two, I could choose to listen to my heart and mind that told me to continue to focus forward on the signs I could see and feel for myself.

I decided to listen to my own instincts. I had been given tender mercies from God that I was healing and I was improving. I decided to listen to that voice and continue to watch for other signs of improvement. I would hold on to this hope. Hope would give me power to continue as I fulfilled my dream. I left with the resolve that I would never fully follow and blindly listen to the experts again, but would instead find out for myself by looking to the one true Expert and then follow the signs that would lead me to my righteous desires. The signs may be small and the improvements may be slow but every time one happens I determined to deposit it immediately into my dream account by writing it down. I've learned no matter how impressive it was or will be, if I don't write it down I will forget what really happened. By doing this, you can look back on past experiences and make mental withdrawals when times become bleak and blurry. Those records of positive experiences can help us get through the tough and rough roads ahead.

I invite you to recognize the tender mercies of the Lord. Be grateful for the improvement, no matter how small it may be. Keep a record of the signs of improvement along your journey. Write in a journal, on the computer, on your phone, or on your gratitude worksheet. It really doesn't matter as long as you look for the signs, recognize them, and write them down. Write 10 things you are grateful for every day for the next 7 days and appreciate the changes you will discover!

Gratitude List

www.griffinmotivation.com/gratitude

Day 1: My Gratitude List

1. _____

2. _____

3. _____

4. _____

5. _____

6. _____

7. _____

8. _____

9. _____

10. _____

Be quiet and still for 5 minutes a day and recognize the tender mercies of the Lord!

MILE MARKER 10

My Best Friends

Mile Marker 10–My Best Friends

By the end of two months I was greeting the nurses and staffers by name. The hospital was almost starting to feel like home. Almost. I was going to miss the nurses, therapists, and medical staff I saw on a daily basis. They became my friends. They taught me how to dress myself and do my own laundry. They did a wonderful job motivating me when I started to slack off. They did an even better job comforting me when I got down and discouraged. They encouraged me to go to group therapy and talk about the new challenges I would be facing. They taught me how to get around in my wheelchair and do wheelies. They occasionally took me outside the hospital and taught me how to adapt to the entertainment and leisure worlds. We went to a movie and had popcorn and treats. We went to a restaurant and enjoyed a hot cooked meal that wasn't prepared from the hospital. I was going to miss them but I was still itching to go home to be with my family and friends.

"Two months in the hospital," I thought. "I made it two months without incident and they're letting me go home early like I wanted!" My daily persistence paid off. I was going home to my family and friends. Someone must have finally cleaned out the suggestion box and found all my letters begging to go home because the doctors were going to discharge me early.

"They actually listened to me," I thought, half dazed and half amazed. There was a comment or suggestion box on the bottom floor of the rehab center. It was right next to the administration offices. Part of my daily ritual was to go down the elevator and write my desire to my doctors and therapists. It went like this, "Let Jeff Griffin GO HOME!" I'm sure the persistency of my suggestions in the box and my comments directly to the doctors on their weekly visits influenced the date of my release and departure. Instead of the planned three months of rehab and recovery, I was getting out an entire month early. I was able to leave the hospital and go home for good, where I would be surrounded by my loved ones and family. I would finally be back with my support team again!

My wounds were healing and my back was getting stronger. I still had to wear my brace but I was starting to figure out how to get around better with it on. I was spending more time out of my bed and more time in my wheelchair. Over the weeks, I started to see the correlation my back brace had with my spiritual recovery as well. I started to piece it together and understand I couldn't heal on my own. In fact, the recovery would be wrong or even damaging if I didn't use this support. I knew true healing and recovery would only happen if I did it the right way and used the correct tools.

Accepting Christ is like putting on a spiritual back brace. We can't be healed on our own and there are damaging consequences if we don't use His grace properly. There is eternal support and healing available if we choose to put it on. I'd felt Him wrap His arms around me and support me and heal me during those last few months. I even believed someday I would eventually be able to take it off and stand on my own and take the path that leads to the top. He had become my very best friend and I never want to disappoint Him.

Doug was one of the very few friends who consistently came down and visited. We would talk about the important things in life. We mostly talked about "this girl" in his psychology class. I would give Doug pointers on how to approach her or how to talk to her so he could get her phone number. It's not like I was the best at getting numbers and having conversations with girls but I knew enough to help

Doug out. Days would go by before Doug would come and visit again. He would bring me updates and give me details of his progress. I was being discharged and would soon be going home. I'd be closer to the action and more available to help but until then his visits helped me more than he knows. He was a great friend. During one of our visits and conversations about Doug's relationship I began to contemplate my own possible future relationships.

Would I ever get married? Why would it be any easier for me now? At times I would find myself down and depressed and begin to think of the worst. Why would someone want to marry someone who is in a wheelchair? I wouldn't want to! How would I provide for her? How would I protect her? How could I give her what I believed she needed? Even though it was long ago, the memory of the mean girls in fifth grade was a hard one to handle and difficult to deal with. I decided if it hadn't damaged me before my accident, and if it hadn't destroyed me after my accident, then I sure wasn't going to let it fully effect my courage and confidence in my future. With that said, I still felt like a full frontal mental attack was bearing down on my mind. Bring it on—I was ready for the challenge. I believed I was well-equipped for this mental battle. I just didn't know it would come through my best friend.

I eventually returned home and it was cold outside. Doug entered our warm home through the front doors, but I'm sure he couldn't feel the weather that day as he shut the door behind him. When he came in he had a huge smile on his face.

"What's up Doug," I asked, knowing he had something to say.

"I got it!"

"Got what?" I asked.

"I got her phone number!"

"Whose?"

"Emily's!"

Emily Joan Hollist was a beautiful, energetic, and emotional young woman. She was full of life and always willing to try something new as long as it fit within the boundaries and standards she set for herself. She was one who never saw my wheelchair. She only saw ME! She finally gave Doug her number and he left immediately to tell me the good news. We celebrated the victory together with a high-five. I was genuinely happy and excited about the future possibilities for him.

My own future came with classes and homework at Utah State University. Winter semester eventually came and I began attending my classes I had signed up for. My new educational journey at USU had begun. Most days were uneventful and this particular day seemed like it was going to be the same as any other day. It was the beginning of the new semester and I was going to my math class. Doug was walking me to class and keeping me company. Emily was coming from her swim class in the opposite direction. Doug nudged me on my shoulder and said, "That's her, that's Emily; the girl in my physiology class."

We both stopped in the middle of the sidewalk as we reached each other. We all said a quick hello and Doug introduced me. I heard a lot about this girl from the hospital reports by my bedside. I looked at her with approval and thought, "She's cute," and nothing else. You see, there is a creed among real friends that you don't go after your best friend's girl. I knew Doug liked this girl and I wasn't going to go after her. After the introductions were over the awkward silence began. We were all standing there waiting for the other to say something more. I finally broke the silence and kept the conversation moving along until we too were obliged to leave for class. When we got far enough away from being overheard,

Doug turned to me and sought my opinion. "So, what do you think?" I knew what he was asking and I told him she was cute. I really didn't think more than that. She had just come from swim class with wet hair and she was the girl of my buddy's dreams. What more could I think?

I knew it wasn't going well for Doug, so as a good friend I encouraged him to set up another "impromptu" meeting in the food court. We just happened to be where Emily was going to be for lunch that day. We sat down in the open where we knew she couldn't miss us. Sure enough, a few minutes after we sat down Emily and her friend showed up. Before they purchased their own food they spotted us. Pleasantries were exchanged before we invited them to sit down and eat lunch with us. I thought for sure this time would be better for Doug but I was wrong. Doug talked more than the last time but said less than he needed to. I was convinced the third time would be the charm.

This time we met outside her apartment. Doug and I stayed in the nice warm car and chatted while Emily shuffled around outside in the cold. It wasn't until after she offered us some homemade bread that we invited her to get inside the warm car and visit for a minute. As she went in her apartment to get the bread she had made on her own, I told Doug he'd better make this count because the stakes just went up. "A woman who can cook is more valuable than a woman who can...," Emily came back before I could finish. By the time our conversation was over, Doug could clearly see what I couldn't. He could tell Emily was interested in me and not him, which is a hard pill to swallow for anyone. I refused to believe or entertain the idea because I knew how much Doug liked this girl and you don't do that to your best friend. Plus, I thought it was impossible for a girl to want to date a guy in a wheelchair.

As we drove away that night, the conversation steered its way back to Emily. "What did you think of the bread," I asked. Before I could finish the word bread, Doug interrupted.

"Griff, she likes you."

I'm sure Doug said what he said out loud in hopes it wouldn't possibly hurt as much as it did in his head. But I also believe he was trying to convince himself, and me, to see what I refused to acknowledge all along.

In confusion and denial I responded, "What are you talking about?"

"You need to ask her out," he continued with pain in his voice.

"I'm not going to do that, Doug," I responded with like conviction. "You like her, and I'm not going to go there. Plus, why would she like someone in a wheelchair?" I still had flash backs from 5th grade and I didn't want to compound those memories from a wheelchair. "Maybe later." Wanting to change the conversation I asked Doug about the current basketball season. "Do the Jazz have a chance this year?" I thought I had dodged a bullet.

Doug and I continued to be friends and he eventually convinced me to ask Emily out, but I felt like I needed to first heal from the wounds of my past. Having relationships before my accident were tough but now they seemed impossible. I knew I couldn't keep looking back to what used to be so I committed to do better and to be more as I began to move forward. I had recommitted myself during those dark and lonely moments in the hospital to do all I was presently doing and then push myself a little bit more. Not just with dating but with all aspects of my life. Before my accident I pushed myself mentally, physically, socially, and spiritually. I tried to do new things that stretched me. It wasn't always easy before but it seemed even more difficult and awkward from a wheelchair. I wanted to be well-balanced in life and I wasn't going to use my wheelchair as an excuse. I believed that meant I needed to improve my abilities with my family, friends, and neighbors in both private and social settings. I needed to heal physically and repair my broken body. I needed to exercise more and eat better. I needed to improve my mental capacities and obtain greater knowledge at school and in life. I also needed to improve my relationship with God. I knew I had to be better with all four categories and I knew the latter would help with the other three automatically.

Before asking Emily out, I felt like I needed to rekindle my relationship with my Heavenly Father. I needed to get my priorities straight. I needed to make Him my best friend. I had abandoned Him for a while and needed to return. I tried to be more consistent with my scripture reading and my daily prayers. It had suffered this last year. It was my fault and I needed to make it right. Not only did I sign up for my college classes on campus, I also signed up for a religion class as well. I was going to prove my love to God and demonstrate my devotion through my actions.

Steady signs of improvement were starting to happen. Hard work was becoming one of my best friends. Consistency with my positive choices was having an impact physically, mentally, spiritually, and socially. The surgical scars were healing and my body was getting stronger. Better grades were evidence my mind and intellect were growing. My spiritual self was seeing signs of improvement too. I was starting to gain confidence again but like my physical body, I still had a long way to go to be made whole. Still, the positive progress I was making with my friends was refreshing.

Revisit your dream bucket list in Mile Marker 2. Are you

in balance? Is most of your focus in one category? In Luke 2:52 we're taught Jesus "increased in wisdom and stature, and in favour with God and man." If we want to have increase we need to be balanced. To become more balanced and a better person I invite you to look at your Life Cycle chart and have a silent self-assessment session about your dreams. Choose one area of improvement in one of the following categories of your life cycle to better balance your life. Write the date and your initials next to the category and list what area you want to work on for the month.

Life Cycle Chart—Download chart at
www.griffinmotivation.com/lifecycle

Physical_____

Mental_____

Social_____

Spiritual_____

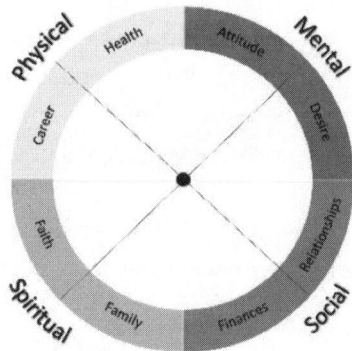

Jeff Griffin
2004 Paralympic
Athens, Greece

2004 Paralympic Games in Athens, Greece.

MILE MARKER 11

Walk Through the Door
& Enjoy the Journey

Mile Marker 11—Walk Through the Door and Enjoy the Journey

Around the Sixth Century B.C.E. Greece had Plato and Socrates, India had the Buddha, and China had Confucius and Lao Tzu. These world philosophers gave us many blocks of truth to build a solid foundation upon for our lives. Many of their teachings ring as true today as they did back then. A specific truth Confucius talked about is about what it takes to arrive at one's destination. He said, "The journey of a thousand miles begins with a single step." Planning for the future eliminates many obstacles but living in the present is essential to enjoying life's journey.

I received the news that I would be going home. I had obtained my goal to leave earlier than planned but I still hadn't accomplished my other goal of walking out of the hospital. I wanted to walk out of the hospital so badly that I had reoccurring dreams at night of running to first base like I once did as a child. I would wake up panting only to find myself back in the hospital. I wasn't scheduled to go home just yet but they were letting me go a month early. The walking would come later, I was sure of that, but I needed to get back home to my support team.

It was early fall and the leaves were changing colors and falling off the trees. Football had just begun and the days were getting shorter. The day of being discharged from the hospital had finally arrived. My parents were there helping me pack my belongings. They cleaned out my nightstand and put my scriptures and journal in the box that would be coming home with me. The cards came down and the flowers were thrown away. They were pretty much dead by this time because

I hadn't received any for weeks. I glanced around the room one last time before rolling out of there for good. I told my roommates goodbye and wished them the best of luck with their own recoveries. With a box on my lap, my parents by my side, and the exit doors in front of me, I was ready for the next adventure.

We exited the front doors and approached the awaiting van with nervous excitement. Jill, my new friend and old therapist, accompanied me out to the van to say goodbye and to make sure I got in safely. I noticed she was carrying a long wooden board in her hands when I asked, "What is that for? Are you going to hit me over the top of my head for your last goodbye?" She was always tough on me but never this rough.

My parents took the box of personal items off my lap and stuck them in the back of the van. "Jeff, you take the front seat," my dad commanded. I accepted the invitation as an honor and opened the passenger door. I positioned my chair as close to the van as possible. I got pretty close but still lacked a large gap between me and the seat. Everyone stepped back and watched me try to get from one seat to the other. This simple obstacle could have discouraged me to the point of frustration if I allowed it to. I first tried the simple transfer technique I learned in my therapy sessions. It didn't work because the gap was too large and the van seat sat higher than my chair.

I assessed the situation and scanned the area for a solution. I noticed the van handle hanging from the ceiling so I reached out to grab it but I couldn't quite reach it without falling out of my chair. Family members became nervous while the therapist sat back and smiled. She knew the personal struggle would give me strength. "Do you want some help with that," she finally asked. A little embarrassed and a lot frustrated I conceded my wounded pride and humbly replied, "Yes, I can use some help."

128

She handed me the wooden board and said, "There you go."

Crinkling my nose and squinting my eyebrows together I asked, "What's this for?"

"It's to help you get from your chair to the van," she replied as if everyone in the world knew what the board was for.

Dubious as before I said, "How can a piece of wood help me get from my chair to the van?"

She let out a long sigh and rolled her eyes one last time and patiently told me how to use the board. She told me to put one end under my rear end, closest to the van, and then place the other end on the seat of the van. I did as she said. Once in place the board made a little plank that bridged the gap that kept me from getting in the van. "Ingenious," I thought. "Who would have thought something this simple and basic could make such a difference?"

With the board securely positioned, I slowly scooted my body across the divide. I arrived safely to the other side without hurting myself. A shower of exuberance enveloped me once I accomplished this seemingly simple task. I was grateful to be in the passenger seat and ready to start my new journey. I turned toward the spectators and thanked my therapist with a giant smile on my face and a little twinkle of gratitude in my eye. We had worked with each other for two months and knew each other very well. She smiled back and said, "This place will never be the same."

"I know, you'll never have somebody like me again," I teased back.

"Thank goodness for that," she said as everybody laughed and got into the van. We both knew what the other really meant. The whole ordeal, of getting from my chair to the van took about 15 minutes.

I thought for sure the prolonged process of doing

everything longer would have driven my dad nuts. He is always ready to get on the road but that day he never said a word about it. My whole life I have tried to follow in his footsteps. My dad's long strides were an indication of his own life. Always going, and going fast. This was the first time I could remember that my dad didn't show any signs of frustration about a delay. He finished putting my chair in the van and as he put the van in reverse to head home, I sat there across from him and hoped I could be as patient and caring to my own son, if I ever had one myself. He never blamed me once or chastised me for cutting corners. He didn't need to. I'm sure he understood I had done both to myself already. As we distanced ourselves from the hospital I couldn't get over the fact I was actually leaving that place forever.

The 80-mile journey from the big city, through Sardine Canyon, and into Cache Valley was the quickest I could remember. The daydream of sleeping in my own bed and being with my friends again helped the time go by faster. I learned that there are two kinds of hours. There is a fast hour and a slow hour. They are both 60 minutes but one seems to go faster than the other! As we pulled into the driveway and before my dad could stop the car, my brother and sisters had run out of the house and into my arms. It was a wonderful reunion.

I thanked them for the banner they had made and hung on the garage door. Without knowing it they were helping me see the positive things in life. They pointed out the fact our neighbors had come over and helped make the entrance to our home accessible by building a carpeted ramp. With this ramp I would be able to roll into my home without assistance. Tears of joy and gratitude welled up in my eyes and eventually spilled over. I was touched by the love and service they showed me.

I went up the ramp, turned the knob, and pushed opened

the door so I could cross the threshold to my new life. I was home! I was back with my family. I was with loved ones and my support team. It felt right, it looked right, it even smelled right. No more sanitized hospital smells, just some good old-fashioned familiar smells.

My grandmother was sitting in her favorite blue reclining rocking chair as I made it through the door and into the front room. This was her favorite place in the house so she could see people come and go. She greeted me with her familiar smile and the twinkle in her eye indicated how happy she was to have me home. I was always Grandma's favorite. At least she made me feel that way. We hugged each other, both from our chairs. Neither of us could get out and stand. Grandma was too old to take care of herself so Mom insisted she stay with us and let the family take care of her. She was also too old to get around anywhere without the aid of her walker, so most days she would just sit in her recliner and greet people as they came and went.

Coming home was the best thing that could have happened to me. It even got better as the days and weeks went by. Friends came over to see me, family members were much nicer to me, and foes, who soon became friends even called or stopped by to see how I was doing. No matter who came to visit it was always enjoyable for me. Without fail the conversation would come back to my legs and how they were doing. Everyone knew my dream was to walk again so they would always inquire. With a smile on my face I would tell them the truth that, "I still don't have any movement…yet." I never made my visitors feel bad about the question because I knew they wanted me to walk as bad as I did.

As the days went by and the visitors slowed down, I found myself waiting around a lot more hoping for the connection in my back to come back so I could walk again. I prayed every night for a miracle to happen only to wake up in the same condition as before, paralyzed. My sights were on the finish line. The finish line was to walk again. I knew I needed a plan to get there and I needed to do something about it. It became clear I was more consumed with the future results at the finish line than I was about enjoying the moments that would get me there. I was so focused and frustrated with the end results that I almost never got started in the first place.

Months had gone by and the weather was starting to warm up and I was getting antsy to do something besides sitting around and hoping for a miracle to happen. Progress was slow during those winter months. Winter finally faded away and the showers of spring washed away the lingering signs of the cold and dreary past. Six months had passed and I still couldn't walk. I thought six months was a reasonable amount of time and that I should be able to walk again. I had regained some movement in my thighs but that was the only improvement I saw. I was tired of waiting around for something to happen. I needed to do more than just wish. Something sparked my desire to do something about it.

One day as I rolled past my grandma I saw her walker from the corner of my eye and heard something that caught my attention. The sight and sound hit me like a ton of bricks. "You should use her walker to help you get out of your chair and out the door." The impression came as clear as a voice. I listened to the prompting and took my grandma's walker from her. I finally saw it as a useful tool. I asked permission to borrow it and she kindly complied, sitting there in her full-body pajamas. I always thought her pink pajamas went well with her bright white hair.

The distance from where Grandma and the walker usually sat was about 10-15 feet from the front door. I positioned the walker so it was right in front of me, handles shoulder-width and eye level. It reminded me of portable parallel bars. Memories of the therapy room came flooding back to my mind as I prepared myself to stand. I scooted forward to the edge of my chair and placed both hands on the rails of the walker. I hoisted my body and the dead weight of my legs to a standing position. I wobbled precariously back and forth while I waited for the room to stop swirling around in circles. I was up and facing the right direction. My goal that day was to make it to the door.

With Grandma watching and cheering me on, I started toward my destination. Like most, this particular journey started with one small step. I tried to lift my leg and extend it the same way we practiced in rehab. It was obviously not the same because I didn't have someone there to pick my leg up and put it down like before. "No problem," I thought to myself. "I'll simply have to adjust my strategy."

Instead of lifting my knee up and extending it forward like an able-bodied person, I would lift my leg up by flexing my hip muscle. Once it was high enough I would swing my leg forward and let my foot flop in front of me. This motion was more of a scoot than a swing but the repeated process helped me make it to the front door. Sweat was dripping from my forehead and my breathing was heavy as I turned to look at the clock to see how long it took me to get there. Thirty minutes! I couldn't believe it. It took me half an hour to go 15 feet. That was about a foot every two minutes. I became even more exhausted now I knew how long it took. I looked at my grandma with pleading eyes as I said, "You don't think you can get my wheelchair for me, do you?" We both knew the answer to that question so it didn't need to be said. I had her walker and she was in a very low and soft reclining chair. I was on my own with this one.

There was no use complaining or feeling sorry for myself because I knew what the solution was. I figured since Grandma couldn't help me and I was able to make it to the door in the first place I could always make it back to my wheelchair. I took a deep breath and dug in deep hoping to find that extra reserve of energy and determination that was stored deep within. I went to that place where you mentally have to fill up on the fumes of fortitude to do something incredibly hard. I took a deep breath and began my journey back to my chair. Sixty minutes later and nearly back to my chair my mom appeared around the corner after coming in from outside. "Mom," I shouted emphatically. I had never been so excited to see my mother than at that moment. "Can you help me?" I continued to plead. She stopped what she was doing and took a few seconds to assess the situation. A quick smile appeared and a girlish giggle escaped as she realized my predicament.

"Yes son, I'll help you," she replied. "What do you want me to do?"

At this moment we both realized I was much more grateful for her help at 22 than I ever was during my teenage years. Mom grabbed my chair and rolled it over to me. Three seconds is all it took and she was by my side. She covered the same distance a thousand times faster than I was capable of doing it myself. I appreciated that simple act of kindness as I relaxed my shoulders, arms, and body and melted into my wheelchair.

My experience that particular day caused me to begin looking at the joys that come with the journey and not just the destination. So often in life I had been caught up with the destination and forgotten about the landscape along the path. I decided I would try to stop and smell the proverbial roses a little more often. I would do this one rose at a time.

After several weeks of scooting back and forth with

Grandma's walker in my living room, I decided to venture outside to see what other encounters I could experience. The first time going outside was exhilarating. When I reached the door, and opened it up I noticed I would have to maneuver down the wheelchair ramp, which in reality was a slight gentle decline. But on that day, the ramp never seemed so steep as it did that moment. It felt like I was staring down the K12 Mountain.

I eventually got the walker wheels over the threshold and onto the ramp. When I got my whole body on the ramp, it felt like I was going to need a runaway truck ramp to slow me down. I made it down the ramp safely, only to face the second ramp that was awaiting and taunting me. There must have been an angel helping me because I made it down the second ramp and traveled the few feet to the driveway. By the time I got to the driveway it was time to turn around. I learned very fast that not only did I need to plan for enough energy and time to get to my desired destination, but I needed twice the amount for the safe return.

It wasn't often I missed a day of old-lady exercises with the walker. I took Sundays off. Every day I would say goodbye to my grandma as I walked through the front door, and every day when I returned I would be greeted by her bright and hearty hello. I loved the companionship of my grandmother. On the most difficult days, when I would go too far or have something unexpected happen, I would enter through the front door and be greeted with a cheerful hello and a slow-motion fist pump or an important question like "Do you need a root beer float?" Grandma believed a good old-fashioned root beer float could fix any problem. "…because it really looks like you need a root beer float," she continued.

"No Grandma, I don't need a root beer float today," I

would continue jokingly, "but I could sure use a hamburger!" A hamburger was her other remedy for ailments. On occasion I would take her up on one of her offers and get one for both of us.

Spring turned into summer and fall was fast approaching. I was venturing off farther and farther from home. I made it from the driveway to the street and wasn't quite sure if I should go left, which was up the street, or turn right and go down it. Either way, the street was pretty flat. I made a choice and went left. There was a stop sign at the end of the street that could be seen when I stood on the edge of the driveway. It was about two blocks away. I decided to go for it. I began like I always did: one step at a time. Occasionally a neighbor would be outside and I would wave or say hello. One time my neighbor told me the first time he saw me going down the street he would have to hold up his hand between me and his line of vision to see if I was really moving. I found that amazing because I thought by this time I was cruising up and down the street with the wind blowing through my hair.

Another time while walking up the same street I was nearing the end of my journey and fast approaching the stop sign. A car with a familiar face inside drove by. We both waved to each other as he drove past me and up the perpendicular street. When I reached the stop sign I took a quick five-minute break to catch my breath before returning home. Before I began the journey back I recognized the same familiar car with the same person inside but this time driving in the opposite direction. The expression on the man's face was priceless. He did a double-take glance as he drove by. He looked concerned as we waved goodbye. His wave looked slow motion to me. Maybe it was because time was moving and I was not. It wasn't until I looked down at my watch that I realized it had taken about thirty minutes, including my five minute break, to finish those last few feet.

It took me several hours to travel from point A to point B. When I first started using the walker all I could focus on was getting to point B. I had blinders on and could only see my destination. I didn't care how long it took or what it would cost my body to get there. I didn't notice what was happening around me, even the stares or glances of concern. It wasn't until I stopped and turned around that I realized how far I had come or what I had accomplished. Reaching the destination was euphoric, but I also noticed I had missed many of the other beauties that could be found along the journey.

I started to slow down, if that was truly possible, and tried to experience the moment a little more. I tried to recognize the heat of the sun on my face and back as I walked up and down the street. It felt warm and rejuvenating. I tried to have a race with the worms that lined the streets after a summer storm. They were one of the few things I could actually beat. I tried to listen to the songs of the birds as they accompanied me along my path. At times it was better than an iPod. I tried to forget about tomorrow, when the miracle of walking might take place, and experience the present while I still had it. The here and now is truly a gift from God; that is why they call it the "present."

I'm glad I walked through the front door and continued my journey. I know I still need to push myself and do something more every day. I know I must continue to dream and plan for the future. I know if I just DOn't quIT and continue to go forward every day one step at a time, I'll eventually arrive where I want to be. The trick is to enjoy the journey and everything that comes with it, otherwise you will have a lot of empty yesterdays.

Vince Lombardi, the Super Bowl coach of Green Bay Packers and namesake of the current trophy said, "Man cannot dream himself into character, but that he must hammer and forge one for himself."[7]

Put down the book, get off the couch, take one step forward, and walk through the door. Oh, and by the way, don't forget to enjoy the journey along the way.

---

[7]Lombardi, V. (2001). *What It Takes To Be #1*, pp. 38-39. New York:, NY: McGraw-Hill.

Get up, Get out, and Get Going

Jeff and Emily posing for the camera.

Defensive coordinator for the champion
Jordan Beat Diggers.

Meeting President George W. Bush.

MILE MARKER 12

Dance! There Really Is
a Happily Ever After

Mile Marker 12–Dance! There Really Is a Happily Ever After

I hate dances! I feel silly, stupid, and awkward. I would prefer staying home than going to a dance. The problem is, the pretty girls like to dance and I wanted to be with the pretty girls. I always felt awkward going to dances because I didn't know how to dance. After being taught how to dance I still felt stupid and tried to convince myself that stepping back and forth and moving side to side was exciting and romantic. That was just with the slow songs. When it came to the fast songs I couldn't find the rhythm and I definitely couldn't find the confidence or the apathy to let loose to the music. One time I made the mistake of imagining the music off while everyone else was dancing. They all looked ridiculous to me.

There was a dance on campus and my friends tried to convince me to go. Why would I put myself through this agony again, especially in a wheelchair? They reminded me–the pretty girls still liked to dance and they would be there that night. "Yeah, but they'll be dancing with other boys while I watch from a wheelchair on the sideline." This thought was my strongest argument but I knew it didn't hold much water. I knew if I didn't go at all there was a 100 percent chance I wouldn't be dancing with the pretty girls. On the other hand, if I did go there would always be a chance of meeting one of them. I agreed to go, not knowing beforehand how it would turn out. I had no idea how I would dance side to side without any legs. I had no clue what to do, especially during a fast song.

As I entered the doors to the dance hall the beat of the music hit me full force and the energy in the air was tangible. Memories and emotions surged through my body and mind and I wanted to turn around and hide. I wanted to leave before I even got there but I mustered the courage, rolled in with my head held high, and convinced myself and others I really wanted to be there. The first two songs were fast and I sat by my friends for protection and comfort. That was a mistake. They quickly pushed me out to the middle of the dance floor. All eyes were on me and I had a choice to make. Start dancing or leave forever. Time stopped for what felt like eternity but I quickly chose to stay and dance. I moved to the rhythm of the beat the best I could. The eyes and stares eventually turned away and I was starting to feel safe again. I could kill my friends for doing that or I could thank them for treating me like a friend and helping me forget about my fears and just dance.

The next song was a slow song. I didn't know many people and I didn't want to break the ice quite yet. I still hadn't figured out how to ask a girl to dance from a wheelchair. I still didn't know how I was going to dance to a slow song even if the girl did say yes. My fears were snuffed out immediately when Emily came out of nowhere and asked me to dance. I told her I didn't know what we would do or how we would dance but I accepted her invitation anyway. I rolled out on to the floor and suggested she sit on my lap while I would move my chair to the music. She gladly accepted and sat on my lap with her arms around my neck. That was one of the quickest slow songs I had ever danced to. The dance finished and I thanked her and went back to my friends.

I did have an awkward moment with Doug. He was right about Emily liking me after all, but I quickly forgot about it because I was stunned and amazed someone would want to dance with me! Someone who couldn't use his legs to move! Someone in a wheelchair! By the end of the night there was literally a line of girls waiting and wanting to dance with me.

142

Before the dance I wasn't able to see the possibilities but Emily showed me a new way, a possible way, a beautiful way. The impossible was turned upside down instantly and became possible. I knew immediately there were girls out there who would want to dance with someone who was different than the masses. My world began to get better that very night and it started by dancing.

The dancing didn't stop there and the impossible became possible on July 10, 1997, when I married the girl of my dreams for time and all eternity. I never thought that day would come. Emily and I have been married now for more than 20 years. I can honestly say I find her more beautiful today than when I first met her. I enjoy being with her and I'm at peace with our relationship. It's not to say we haven't had any hard times or differences. In fact, we've probably had more than the average couple.

I believe marriage was ordained of God and if you allow Jesus to touch your marriage it will live. If you let Him touch your life, it will live. I even believe if you let Him touch your job, school, or play it will live. Whatever Jesus touches lives! Emily and I have tried to live by that belief and work at it every day. We haven't been perfect with our relationship and at times we've even wanted to quit. Have you ever wanted to quit or give up? Don't! No matter what you do, don't make quitting an option. From the beginning Emily and I made staying together our number one priority, no matter the cost.

That which is important to us we'll choose for ourselves, but that which is not important to us others will choose for us. We need to decide today what's important to us tomorrow and then find a way to do it immediately.

I learned if we don't fix our sights on something or stay focused long enough on what we really want, we will eventually get lost from what we truly desire. Emily and I didn't want to lose each other so we chose to work out a way to resolve our differences when they appeared. Fortunately, they appeared often. That might sound counterintuitive, but we found there is strength in the struggle. I'm not suggesting you try to find problems. You don't have to do that because there are already enough problems that come with a marriage. You just have to have perspective.

When things get really tough, Emily and I take a quick step back from the action. We attempt to catch our breath, take a moment, slowly inhale, and calm our emotions for a while. We give ourselves a time out. It's easier said than done but it's essential. Looking back, I can see the hurdles and obstacle we had to overcome. There were many and some seemed impossible. It was difficult most of the times, even scary at others, but it we knew it would be well worth it in the end. I've learned we can't do it on our own. We must never give up but keep moving forward. We must continue putting one foot in front of the other and look up. If we do these small and simple things we will eventually find the light at the end of the tunnel.

Emily and I dated for a year-and-a-half before we got married. We were on-again off-again two or three times during our relationship. Between her being so young and me being so stupid, it almost never happened. The cards were stacked against me as well. Emily's family liked her other boyfriends more than me, I didn't have a job, and I was going to be in a wheelchair the rest of my life. How was I supposed to provide and protect? It wasn't until a late-night self-evaluation interview that I realized I expected perfection from both of us. I knew I wasn't perfect but Emily was nearly there so I proposed and married her before she could change her mind.

My wife always wanted four or six children. She didn't

care which but she just wanted an even amount. She was in a hurry to have them but I was content to wait a while. I knew once they came I would no longer have her full attention, so I convinced her to wait a year or two so we could get to know each other better and enjoy personal one-on-one time together without any distractions.

We enjoyed the happy and the rough moments together; both helped us become stronger. Each year became better, brighter, and more blissful because we consistently worked at it. We have a simple routine that works for us. Every night before going to bed we pray together. Throughout our marriage we've only missed a dozen times. Our prayerful pleadings were humbling for both of us. It was hard to stay angry with one another after witnessing the other pour out their heart and soul to God. Praying every night was a perfect way to communicate heart to heart. Monday through Friday we would also read the scriptures together. We would read a chapter and talk about what we thought or felt about the words we had just read.

Saturday was date night. We tried to go out at least once a week. Date night has changed over the years but we continue to try and go out alone or with another couple at least once a week. This simple routine has strengthened our marriage. Our dates don't have to be elaborate or expensive either. Some nights it would just be a snow cone or a walk in the woods or a picnic in the park. However, most weeks it would be an evening at a restaurant. Growing up I was the fifth out of eight and the only time we ate at a restaurant was when one of us got baptized or when Dee's had their 10 hamburgers for a dollar deal. On the other hand, my wife was the last out of two and apparently had seen the insides of a restaurant more often than me.

Our worlds were much different growing up and we had

to come together on what was right for us. The counsel given from the Bible in the second chapter of Genesis makes more sense to me now that I'm married when it says that, "a man shall leave his father and mother, and shall cleave unto his wife." We both needed to leave the traditions of our childhood behind and form our own. That was exactly what we were doing with our date nights. We were working at making our marriage an eternal union, a marriage that would last a life time. I've grown to realize that eating a meal or two away from home in a month is cheaper than marriage counsel and divorce.

On Sundays we would read a marriage book. We first started with Dr. Gray's book, *Men Are from Mars, Women Are from Venus*. We found if we were reading it together and came across an issue that personally affected either one of us we could stop and say, "That's exactly how I feel." Or, "That's what you do, too." It was a neutral playing field for us. It wasn't either one of us saying it because Dr. Gray said it in his book. We didn't need to get defensive and end up having an argument. It was safe for us and we felt like we were having our own personal marriage counseling session. We've worked hard at our marriage because we believe it can be a happily ever after marriage after all.

The time arrived in our relationship when it felt right to try to have children. Unfortunately, that baby-making function doesn't work properly for a paralyzed person. I'd heard horror stories from my wheelchair buddies about how they had to try and conceive children. It ranged anywhere from combining their sperm with a donor's to having it shocked out of them with electricity to having it medically removed and then after the egg and sperm were combined it was manually injected back into their spouse. Every method was expensive and not guaranteed to work. It seemed so intrusive to me. My wife and

I decided we were first going to try to experiment on our own and then take it from there.

This time of trial and error with infertility was so difficult for both of us. Our faith was tested, our resolve had to be reassessed, and it pushed the parameters of the possibilities. Month after month our hope would be renewed and rise like the dawn of a new day, believing this would be the month our dreams would be fulfilled. However, month after month our dreams would be shattered and snuffed out like the setting of the sun. Nothing was working and we were both getting frustrated and losing faith. We thought we may never have children and that it would be impossible to have children naturally. We could always go the medical route but there weren't any guarantees there either.

One night while reading the scriptures together we came across the 58th chapter of Isaiah. It talks about a principle that is generally untested and seldom tried: fasting. We discovered a sliver of light and hope in those verses. We knew instantly if we truly desired a child we had to do more than just pray and read the scriptures for heavenly help. We knew what we had to do. We knew we had to fast for this child and allow the Lord to console our afflicted souls. I understand not all desires are obtained immediately or even in this lifetime. Some take longer than others but I believe all righteous desires do eventually come true. It took Abraham many years before his desires were answered but Isaac eventually came and brought joy and happiness to Sarah and him. Fortunately for us, Emily and I didn't have to wait as long as Abraham and Sarah did. In fact, a month later we found out we were going to have a baby. Our wish was about to be fulfilled.

We were sitting in a restaurant enjoying the company of some friends during a tennis tournament in Colorado. We finished our food and decided to top off our meal with some brownies and ice cream, Emily's favorite. After taking two bites of it she was finished. She pushed it away in disgust and said, "This is nasty." I knew something was up because Emily never thinks dessert is nasty. Although I noticed something was different, I still wasn't clued in she might be pregnant. Still another clue was given later that evening. My once protective and gentle touch brought pain to her now. We both still had no idea she could be pregnant and it wasn't until the ride home when the sweetest experience took place for both of us. As we were driving home a simple but sure thought entered my mind and told me we were going to have a baby boy. It was so real and so clear that I turned to Emily and said, "We're going to have a baby!" She too knew instantly we were going to have a baby as soon as I said it. We cried and laughed at the new possibilities.

We weren't supposed to be able to have any children because of my paralysis. Looking back, it doesn't seem like a big deal. At the moment it was huge. But in reality, it was a big deal all along and it still is. It wasn't supposed to happen without help from the experts but it did happen because of the help that came from the true Expert. This modern miracle happened three more times. The last one took a little longer, with a miscarriage in-between. Bradley, Savanna, Karlee, and Katelyn bring great joy to our lives. Some days we want to pull our hair out and scream but most days we find happiness and satisfaction in teaching our own children the importance of having faith in Christ, hoping for a better day, consistently working hard, helping each other out, and doing what is right so they too might have a better life—a happily ever after life!

The definition of an insanity is to do the same thing over and over again and expect different results. If there is doubt and fear in your life that is hindering you from receiving your blessings, I invite you to take that first step of faith forward. Shake off the shackles that weigh you down and just dance. Listen to the music inside your heart and get on the dance floor of life and move!

ABCs and 123s
www.griffinmotivation.com/goals

No success can compensate for failure in the home.

Summit–New Beginnings

Most endings are happy, others are sad, and a few are neither happy nor sad. I've always hoped for a fairytale ending to this story. I imagine it ending with me getting out of my chair and permanently leaving it behind. Someday it will happen but until then I'm going to continue living life. I'm not going to sit around waiting for this miracle to happen only to find out life has passed me by. Instead, I'm going to attack the world one day at a time, discover as many natural and spiritual beauties as possible, and begin a different adventure as often as I can.

I would love to conclude this story with a spectacular ending. The only problem with this concept is it hasn't ended at all. In fact, it has only just begun. When I thought my life was over and my dreams shattered along with my back I had no idea it really wasn't the end of an old dream but instead it was a beginning to a different and better one. Growing up I always believed every story had an ending but I've discovered most endings are just the beginning to another story. When I grow old and eventually die I will make this concept permanent by writing it in stone. My tombstone will read, "Here lies Jeffrey Allen Griffin whose life hasn't really ended but truly has just begun."

Death will not be the end for us but just another hurdle we must jump over in life. Most people fear death and what it represents. The fear of death and the unknown paralyzes our decisions. Fear keeps us from accomplishing many of the things we would otherwise accomplish. Think back to the last time you wanted to venture out and do something different or discover something new but didn't have the courage to do it. It might have been fear of something horrible that kept you from doing it. Death is the ultimate end-all so I believe you really can't live life fully until you have come to grips with the reality of it. I got firsthand knowledge of this concept when I stared death in the eyes when I was stranded in the backcountry of the Uintah National Forest shortly after my accident.

It was a beautiful wintery day. The sun was shining down in the valley and the mountains were calling for me and my friends to go snowmobiling. My two friends and I obeyed the call, hitched up the snowmobiles, and headed to the snow-covered mountains. We unloaded the snowmobiles off the trailer and checked the machines for any problems. Finding nothing wrong with the machines we each jumped on our own machines and raced off into the great white adventure land. We were climbing up hills and racing across wide open fields. One would lead while the other two would try to keep up. Throughout the day we saw spectacular views that would take your breath away. Those vistas were only discovered and viewed by first riding through some treacherous terrain.

The day was going great until somebody decided to follow a single snowmobile trail downhill. We didn't even stop to think that maybe our snowmobiles weren't powerful enough to get back up the hill. When we got halfway down and decided it was getting too rough to follow we turned our sleds around and tried to go back up. Every one of us buried our sleds waist deep into the powdery snow as we pressed down on the accelerator. It was obvious we couldn't go up so we turned around and continued to follow the tracks downhill. We eventually got to a place where the tracks went back up the mountain. Our machines were unable to duplicate them so we continued down the hill using a different route. The mountain continued to force us down into the bottleneck area. We couldn't go left or right because the mountain was too steep to climb. The ravine we were in split the mountain in two. Our choices were limited and we believed we had to enter the ravine hoping it would lead us to safer and calmer terrain. Our hope was in vain. We were going over 10-foot boulders and getting our machines stuck every 5 feet. It was getting dark and we had to make a decision. Either we stay by our machines and wait for help that probably wouldn't come until the next day or climb out of our mess. We chose the latter.

One of my companions took off to go get help while the other helped me up the mountain. I crawled on my hands and knees up the steep ravine, swam through a light powdery sea of snow on the plateau, and collapsed from exhaustion after making our way through a forest of pine trees to the edge of a vast and empty field. We covered the .6 miles of terrain in six hours. During that time and throughout my journey I was challenged both physically and mentally beyond my capacities. Because I was so exhausted and the climb looked so daunting, I wanted to sit down and wait. I was not only fighting the hill but I was also fighting the elements. One minute I was sweating and hot and the next minute I was cold and wet. After four hours into it, every time we passed a tree I would longingly wish to take a nap. My buddy knew if I did I wouldn't wake up, so he insisted I keep moving forward.

My mind was spent and my body was rejecting my personal commands to continue. I started to hallucinate and really thought I wasn't going to make it. The idea was very inviting. What was once so frightful and scary wasn't a big deal to me. I looked death straight in the eyes and was no longer afraid of it. But death was a big deal to my pregnant wife, who was expecting our first child, and it would have destroyed her. Between the thought of hurting my wife and the constant encouragement from my friend I continued to fight the demons of despair. Help eventually arrived and I was rescued and returned to safety so I could live another day.

That near-death experience was another of life's paradoxes that helped me begin to truly live life both freer and fuller. Our mortal existence will eventually come to an end for all of us. We must understand it, embrace it, and accept it before we can fully begin to live it and enjoy it. If not, we will constantly be looking over our shoulders with fear. We will be hesitant to act, unwilling to push, and unable to stretch the limits that will increase our capacity to conquer. We will be powerless and paralyzed to take bold and calculated risks. We must face our fears and fan the flames of faith. We must courageously continue forward and believe in a better day.

I believe my story and experiences parallel our lives in one aspect or another. It started from nowhere and has developed into something that is now here. If you look a little closer at the last sentence you will see the only difference in the two phrases of nowhere and now here is a little space and time. This beautiful concept of where we have come from and where we are now can be obtained by taking it one step at a time, a little bit at a time.

I wish I could say I can walk without aid, but I can't, at least not yet. Some people ask me whether or not I would do it differently if I had a chance. Or if I could go back would I change things. The answer is always the same. I tell them I am honestly grateful I am in a wheelchair. They look at me in disbelief while cocking their head slightly to one side or the other trying to process the response. They have a hard time believing I am being sincere. What I don't tell them is they are asking the wrong question. If I had a do-over I would obviously make some changes. I would have rented a lift to paint the high parts of the barn. If I couldn't rent a lift I would have harnessed myself with a climbing rope. Or I would have put the scaffolding closer to the barn so it wouldn't have tipped over. Like I mentioned before, hindsight is 20/20 and I don't have the luxury to go back. The reality is I can't go back and have a do-over and it doesn't matter because now I've arrived where I am today and become the person I am today I wouldn't change anything. I know I'm on the right path and if I continue to improve on the things I am doing today, mistakes will be erased, limits will be removed, and excuses will be obsolete.

I've been given an opportunity to share a few things I've learned from this particular experience in my life. My accident, which many think was tragic, has taken me places and allowed me to do things I couldn't have imagined before it. Most of the things I've done and experienced would have been impossible before. But the impossible has become possible.

I've traveled the world and explored new cultures and discovered the beauty that is found in other countries. I've played for a national championship wheelchair basketball team and know what it's like to compete at the highest level. I've played on a team where expectations were high and unity was low so we played much lower than our potential and lost terribly. We came away dejected and embarrassed.

I've had the opportunity to run the St. George marathon, or better yet, roll the St. George marathon. There were places along the 26.2 mile course that would take your breath away but crossing the finish line in first place leaves you speechless. The vistas along the course were spectacular. It was such an up and down experience. There were parts of the course that were so steep going up it took everything you had to push and will yourself to the top. While on the opposite end of the spectrum there were parts of the course that were so steep coming down you would reach speeds up to 55 miles per hour. Being so close to the road while traveling that fast is an insane and thrilling experience I will never forget.

I've played for the wheelchair NBA All-Star Team and been selected as the Most Valuable Player four out of the eight years I played. I've competed in world events like the Paralympics in Athens, Greece. I've received two world records and gotten my name in the Guinness Book of World Records. I've had the chance to visit the White House on Pennsylvania Avenue and get my picture taken with the president of the United States of America. I've gone on hikes in the National Parks in my wheelchair and experienced immense beauty while getting an upper body workout. I've been in the waters of Utah skiing, fishing, and boating. I've been in the snow-covered mountains snowmobiling and skiing. I've rafted down the whitewater rapids of the Snake River in Wyoming. I've gone places and have done things others thought were impossible.

I've had the privilege to meet and marry the girl who deserves to be as happy as I can make her. We have a little family and serve in our community making a small difference for others. Would I change any of that for a do-over? Not on your life.

I still have dreams of doing great things and becoming someone special. I haven't stopped wishing for wonderful things to do and be. My desires are more genuine and I'm doing a better job at focusing more on the important things of life. I've got a long way to go before I accomplish a lot of those dreams but for the moment I understand how to get there.

Occasionally my ego gets in the way of what I really need to do and become. Don't get me wrong, I believe we can accomplish some great things on our own. History has shown that. We can do a lot of wonderful things and help out a lot of people on our own. We can climb high, run fast, play hard, or anything else we dream about. But if we do it on our own we will only get so far. We all have a great purpose in this life whether it is big or small to others. All of us can find our quests if we simply connect with the source that can make it all happen. When we take advantage of all the resources around us we will fully learn to live and be successful. We must increase our will and desire to connect with that source on a daily basis through prayer and meditation. It will help us overcome our ego, elevate us to a better level, and realign our intentions with God's.

I've been practicing this process every day since my accident. God is the real source that has helped me turn the impossible into the possible. He has helped me see the good in all things. There is so much good out there, even amongst the chaos. If you only look for it you will find it. It takes daily reminders to help us accomplish this task of resisting the frictions and distractions of life but I know it's possible. In fact, impossible becomes possible when we invite the great I AM into our lives.

Personal sacrifice is needed to overcome the selfishness in our lives. Everything good requires effort. Effort is increased when we do what is right. When we do what is right, the light in our lives increases. Light is power and this, in return, helps us recognize the good in all things, which gives us the strength necessary to do what is right. When we do what is right it makes everything and everyone around us better. If everyone did this, we would live in greater peace and harmony and experience true joy and happiness. This joy and happiness will spread throughout the land the more we do right and the more we love others. It will be like an expanding funnel, similar to a tornado that gets bigger and wider as it rises in the sky. The more right-for-us (righteous) decisions we make in our lives the higher we go and the bigger we become. If we set aside our egos and turn our lives over to God, He can do more with us and take us to brighter heights and more beautiful vistas than we could ever do on our own.

I'm still progressing and learning how to succeed with what others call a disability. I call it an ability and can honestly say I'm grateful it happened to me. It's changed my vision and how I look at life. Today, I see things clearer and at a higher level! This may seem ironic or a paradox to some, but I truly do see things more clearly. I always see the good things around me when I focus only on them. When I intentionally look for them I see the good even during the most difficult times of my life. The secret is to prepare the best you can for those difficult times that will continue to come but to focus more fully on the positive and good things that accompany the tough times. It's impossible to focus on both.

I invite you to try one last challenge by writing down everything that is good in your life on a sheet of paper and then writing everything that is bad on a separate sheet of paper.

Priorities Principle

More than likely, one list is longer than the other. Now that both the good and the bad lists have been written and examined you have a choice to make. You can pick up the good list or you can pick up the bad list and bring it as close to your eyes as possible while still being able to read it. Whichever list you have chosen to focus on makes it impossible for the other list to be seen. Whether you choose to focus on the longer list or the smaller list, you can only focus on one at a time. You must choose a list to focus on. I choose to focus on the positive and good one!

Nobody is perfect. We all make mistakes, and some make more than others. One of the steps to success is to minimize those mistakes. I understand life, school, work, and even play can be cruel and unfair for whatever reason. We don't always know what problems will come our way. We ourselves are the cause for most of our problems in life. In order to minimize those problems we need to establish solid routines and consistent habits to build a foundation of truth, wisdom, and knowledge to maximize our success. The more we eliminate the distractions and the quicker we create these routines the easier it will be to focus on what matters. We can learn from our mistakes or from the mistakes of others or continue to ignore them and make the same silly decisions that hinder our progression. When we do mess up, which we all will, we must never give up and quit but get back up and try to be better the next time. Whether we are fast learners or not, we can succeed if we DOn't quIT.

Our capacity to gain knowledge and truth is essential to minimize our mistakes and maximize our chances for success. We must put aside the excuses we use as crutches and ignore the disapproving, disparaging, and destructive voices that paralyze our minds and hearts. Shame, blame, and justification keep us below the line where we dwell in doom and gloom. That three-headed monster keeps us from progressing and prospering above the line. Daily prayer and meditation can help us overcome these obstacles and help us live above the line. Taking charge, being accountable, and being responsible for our choices will enable us to live above the line and succeed.

The actual summit of Mount Everest took Hillary and Norgay days to accomplish but the journey took years and years of perspiration and preparation. Perhaps some of your dreams have been challenged. Maybe you have been told you can't get that job you've always wanted. It's possible you've been told, by others or yourself, that you can't lose weight and you believe it. Maybe you've tried and failed on several occasions to quit smoking or drinking so you're convinced you can't. Maybe you've been told or think you can't get a date or maintain a relationship. It's possible you've been told you can't make the team so you don't even try. Perhaps you believe you can't change because that is who you are. Whatever your impossible is, you're living under your potential with shame, blame, and justification.

So, what is your dream? I will not laugh at it. In fact, I invite you right now to open up your mind and believe in it. What is it you want most? Are you scared to even say it out loud? Are you scared that you need the reassurance of others and you doubt they will give it? Worse, will they ridicule your dream? Do you even know where to start? Have you let your own disability destroy your dreams?

Don't let doubt and fear paralyze your dreams. I believe we all have disabilities on some level of our lives. It may be physical where others may or may not see it. Your disability may be a social disability that keeps you from experiencing and enjoying the beauty and joys of the social scene. Your disability may be mental, which can trickle down on all levels of your life and challenge you in more ways than one. Your disability may be spiritual. You may not be able to connect with your inner soul right now. Whatever your disability may be I know you can overcome it if you understand we truly are royalty of a heavenly being and destined for greatness.

You can overcome and conquer your challenges if you believe there is unseen power above to tap into. You can gain additional strength when you rise above the clouds so you

160

can see where you want to go. This knowledge can give you strength to overcome the impossible and make it possible. When you Desire, Dream, and DO and never quIT even when adversity comes your way you can be successful one step at a time. *You're Possible!*

A Thought away from Changing Your Life
www.griffinmotivation.com

I invite you to read this journey again and again, looking for hidden gems you may have missed and left behind the first time. In fact, invite a friend to experience this future journey with you. Enjoy the journey together!

Until we meet again at the top–

Namaste,

About the Author

J eff Griffin knows how to win. He has a master's degree in education. He played in the 2004 Paralympic Games in Athens, Greece. He holds two Guinness Book of World Records and is a four-time National Wheelchair Basketball Association All-Star MVP. He enjoys mentoring youth, distributing wheelchairs in third-world countries, and giving hope to others through his humanitarian efforts with LDS Charities. Jeff married his best friend and together they have four beautiful children. He is passionate about progress!

Look for Jeff's new book coming soon:
Endless Possibilities: 90-day recipe for world record results

www.facebook.com/griffinmotivation
www.griffinmotivation.com